Inside Wall Street's Matching Engine

How Exchanges, Auctions, and Order Routers Actually Work

Victor Trex

Published by NobleTrex Press

For permissions and other inquiries, write to:
P.O. Box 3132, Framingham, MA 01701, USA

Contents

Introduction

To the casual observer, the financial market is an abstraction-a ticker tape scrolling along the bottom of a television screen, a jagged line on a charting application, or a chaotic floor filled with shouting traders. However, the shouting men in colorful jackets are largely ghosts of a bygone era. Today, the modern stock market is essentially software. It is a distributed system of colossal complexity, where the "floor" is a server rack in a New Jersey data center, and the "auctioneer" is a deterministic matching engine executing millions of lines of code per second.

When a trader presses a button to buy shares, they initiate a sequence of events that is equal parts economics, physics, and computer science. The gap between the decision to trade and the confirmation of a trade is measured in microseconds, yet within that fleeting window, an order must traverse a labyrinth of gateways, risk checks, routing algorithms, and priority queues. *Inside Wall Street's Matching Engine* is written to illuminate that dark space between the click and the fill. It is not a book about fundamental analysis, nor is it a guide to picking stocks based on earnings reports. Rather, it is an architectural blueprint of the machine itself.

To understand how prices are discovered, one must first master the vocabulary of the venue. We begin by mapping the landscape of liquidity, distinguishing between the "lit" exchanges where orders are displayed to the world, and the alternative trading systems or dark pools where institutional intent remains hidden. We define the atomic units of the market-orders and quotes-and examine how market participants, from retail investors to high-frequency market makers, express their diverse urgencies through specific order instructions.

At the heart of this text lies the "black box": the matching engine. We strip away the mystique to reveal a strict logical processor. Here, we explore the Limit Order Book, not as a theoretical concept, but as a data structure that must manage state, prioritize competing interests, and execute trades with absolute determinism. We examine the rules of the road-specifically Price-Time priority-and how the engine handles the complex choreography of cancellations, modifications, and aggressive liquidity removal.

While the continuous double auction drives most of the trading day, the market relies on specific moments of convergence to open and close. We therefore dedicate significant attention to the auction mechanisms-the mathematical processes that aggregate fragmented interest to solve for a single, equilibrium price. Furthermore, we acknowledge that a matching engine does not exist in a vacuum; it must broadcast its reality to the world. We explore the physics of market data, the inevitable latency between an event and its observation, and the nuances of the "tape" that can sometimes mislead the uninitiated.

Finally, we trace the journey of an order before it even reaches the exchange. In a fragmented marketplace, the Smart Order Router (SOR) is the unsung hero, navigating a web of fees, rebates, and liquidity pools to satisfy the mandate of Best Execution. By synthesizing these technical elements into practical scenarios, we aim to transform the reader's understanding of execution quality.

The market is neither a casino nor a random walk; it is a structure built on rules, logic, and incentives. Whether you are a quantitative developer, a trader seeking to minimize slippage, or a student of market microstructure, understanding the mechanics of the matching engine is the only way to truly understand the price on your screen. Welcome to the machine.

Chapter 1

The Language of the Market: Orders, Venues, and Participants

Before we can open the hood of a matching engine to see how the gears turn, we must first learn the language it speaks. Modern trading is no longer defined by shouting men in colorful jackets; it is a silent, high-speed conversation between algorithms across a fragmented landscape of server farms. This chapter decodes that conversation, mapping out the hidden venues where money moves, defining the exact difference between a 'quote' and an 'order,' and introducing the diverse cast of characters-from retail day traders to high-frequency market makers-who bring the market to life.

1.1 The Landscape of Trading Venues

When most people imagine the stock market, they visualize a specific physical location: the chaotic trading floor of the New York Stock Exchange (NYSE) as seen in Hollywood movies, or perhaps the sleek, digital ticker tape of Times Square. The mental model is one of a single, centralized gathering place—a town square where all buyers and sellers meet to haggle over the price of a share.

In modern finance, this image is a myth. There is no single "stock market." Instead, the market is a fragmented, decentralized network of disparate computer servers housed in data centers, primarily scattered across northern New Jersey. When you press "buy" on your brokerage app, your order does not necessarily travel to the famous building on Wall Street. Depending on the size of your trade, your broker's routing logic, and the specific stock you are buying, your order might end up in one of nearly fifty different venues.

This phenomenon is known as **market fragmentation**. Just as you can buy a specific brand of coffee at a large supermarket, a boutique bodega, or directly from a wholesaler, you can buy a share of Apple or Microsoft at several different types of venues. Understanding the "plumbing" of the market requires us to map this geography and distinguish between the three primary categories where trades actually occur: "Lit" Exchanges, "Dark" Pools (Alternative Trading Systems), and Wholesalers.

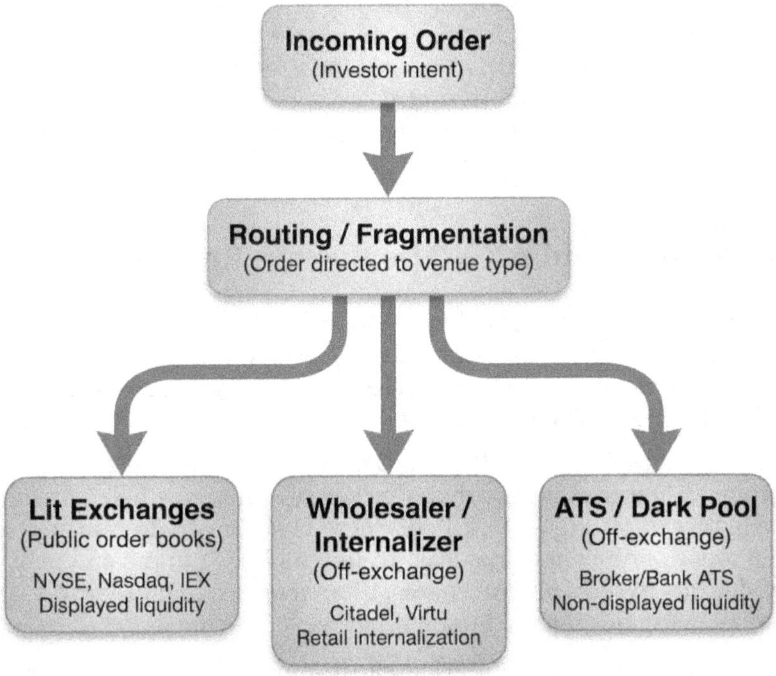

Lit Exchanges: The Public Square

The most familiar venues are the **Lit Exchanges**. These include the heavyweights like the New York Stock Exchange (NYSE) and Nasdaq, as well as challenger exchanges like IEX or Cboe.

They are called "lit" because they operate with **pre-trade transparency**. In a lit exchange, the "lights are on." Every participant can see the available supply and demand before a trade happens. If a pension fund wants to sell 500 shares of a stock at $100.00, that offer is broadcast immediately to the entire world. This transparency creates a universal reference point for the price of a stock.

Lit exchanges act as the official record-keepers of the market. They are heavily regulated and are required to display the "National Best Bid and Offer" (NBBO), essentially the single best price available across all public exchanges at any given microsecond. However, this transparency comes with a cost: information leakage. If you walk into a crowded room and shout that you are desperate to buy a massive amount of gold, the sellers in the room will immediately raise their prices.

Dark Pools and ATS: The Private Rooms

To solve the problem of information leakage, institutional investors, such as mutual funds and pension systems that trade millions of shares at a time, often turn to **Alternative Trading Systems (ATS)**, colloquially known as **Dark Pools**.

Contrary to their ominous name, Dark Pools are not utilized for illicit activity. They are simply private exchanges where the lights are effectively turned off. In a Dark Pool, there is no pre-trade transparency. The order book is not broadcast to the public. If that same pension fund wants to sell 1 million shares, they can place that order in a Dark Pool without alerting the broader market.

The matching engine in a Dark Pool sits quietly, waiting for an opposing order to arrive. If a buyer enters the pool matching the seller's criteria, the trade executes silently. The rest of the market only finds out about the trade *after* it has occurred (post-trade transparency). This allows large investors to move massive amounts of capital without causing the price to skyrocket or crash against them before they finish their trade.

Wholesalers: The Retail Lane

The third category is **Wholesalers** (also known as Internalizers). If you trade stocks using a retail brokerage app on your phone, your order is rarely sent to the NYSE or a Dark Pool. Instead, it is likely routed to a wholesaler—a high-speed electronic trading firm.

Wholesalers operate somewhat like a private concierge for retail orders.

They pay brokers for the right to handle your order (a practice called Payment for Order Flow), and in exchange, they promise to execute your trade at a price that is as good as, or slightly better than, the best price currently displayed on the lit exchanges.

Wholesalers do this by trading against their own inventory. If you want to buy, the wholesaler sells to you from their own stock; if you want to sell, they buy from you. They are willing to do this because retail flow is generally considered "uninformed", meaning a typical individual investor isn't likely to know something about a company's future that the professional market doesn't already know. This makes it safer for wholesalers to trade with individuals than with large, shark-like hedge funds.

A Unified Ecosystem

While these venues operate with different rules and incentives, they are tightly interconnected by high-speed data lines and complex routing algorithms. A single large order might be chopped up by a computer program (a "Smart Order Router"), with pieces sent simultaneously to the NYSE, a Dark Pool, and several other exchanges to find the best possible execution.

Understanding this landscape is the first step in demystifying the matching engine. The engine's behavior depends entirely on where it sits: a matching engine at the NYSE prioritizes public display and regulatory adherence, while a matching engine in a Dark Pool prioritizes secrecy and size. In the next section, we will examine the specific language these engines use to communicate: the precise definitions of orders, quotes, and spreads.

1.2 Core Vocabulary: Orders, Quotes, and Spreads

Having mapped the physical and virtual geography of the market-from the lit exchanges of New York to the silent servers of dark pools-we must now learn the language spoken within them. While the venues may differ, the fundamental vocabulary of electronic trading remains universal. To understand how a matching engine works, we must first understand the atomic units it manipulates: the order, the quote, and the empty space between them known as the spread.

The Order and the Quote

In everyday conversation, investors often use the terms "order" and "quote" interchangeably, but to a matching engine, they represent two distinct states of existence.

An **Order** is an instruction sent by a participant to a venue. It is a kinetic message, an action. It says, "I want to buy 100 shares of Apple," or "I want to sell 500 shares of Microsoft." When you press the "Buy" button in your brokerage app, you are generating an order.

A **Quote**, by contrast, is static. It is a resting advertisement. When an order arrives at an exchange and does not execute immediately, it posts to the electronic ledger known as the **Order Book**. Once it sits there, visible to the market, it becomes a quote. It says, "I am here, waiting to buy at this specific price."

Think of the market like a real estate listing. The "For Sale" sign in the yard with a listed price is the **Quote**-it is an advertisement of intent. The contract an interested buyer submits to purchase the house is the **Order**. The transaction only happens when the order meets the quote.

The Bid and the Ask

The matching engine organizes these resting quotes into two opposing stacks: the Bids and the Asks.

The **Bid** represents the buyers. Specifically, the "Best Bid" is the highest price anyone is currently willing to pay for a stock. If you want to sell your shares immediately, this is the price you will receive.

The **Ask** (or Offer) represents the sellers. The "Best Ask" is the lowest price anyone is currently willing to accept for their stock. If you want to buy shares immediately, this is the price you must pay.

This creates a fundamental tension. Buyers naturally want to pay the lowest possible price, while sellers want to receive the highest. Consequently, the Best Bid is always lower than the Best Ask. If the Bid were ever equal to or higher than the Ask, a trade would occur instantly, and those orders would disappear from the book.

The Spread: The Cost of Immediacy

The gap between the highest price a buyer offers (the Best Bid) and the lowest price a seller accepts (the Best Ask) is called the **Spread**.

For example, if the Best Bid for a stock is $100.00 and the Best Ask is $100.05, the spread is 5 cents.

New investors often view the stock price as a single number, but in reality, a stock always has two prices. The spread represents the **cost of immediacy**. If you want to enter the market *right now*, you must cross the spread. You buy at the higher Ask price and sell at the lower Bid price. That difference is the friction or "toll" paid to the market makers who provide the service of always being ready to trade.

Defining Liquidity

Finally, these concepts aggregate into the most vital characteristic of any market: **Liquidity**.

In popular media, liquidity is often confused with volume (how many shares trade per day). However, in microstructure, liquidity is defined by *resilience*. It answers the question: "How much stock can I buy before I push the price up?"

A "liquid" market is deep. It has thousands of shares available at the Best Bid and Best Ask, and thousands more just a penny away. You can throw a large order into a liquid market like a pebble into an ocean; the surface barely ripples.

An "illiquid" or "thin" market is shallow. There may be only a few shares available at the current price, with the next available shares priced significantly worse. A large order in an illiquid market is like doing a cannonball into a bathtub-the water (price) is displaced violently.

Understanding this vocabulary is a prerequisite for understanding the matching engine. The engine does not "set" prices; it simply acts as the impartial arbiter that manages these stacks of Bids and Asks, continuously calculating the spread and testing the depth of liquidity with every microsecond that passes.

1.3 Expressing Intent: Order Types and Instructions

If the order book is the vocabulary of the market, and the spread is its grammar, then *order types* are the sentences traders speak. Until a trader sends an order, their desire to buy or sell is just a thought—invisible and irrelevant to the market. To turn that desire into a transaction, they must translate their intent into a strict, digital format that the matching engine can understand.

The matching engine is a literalist. It does not understand nuance, hope, or fear. It understands only instructions. And fundamentally, every instruction a trader sends is a negotiation between two competing desires: **immediacy** and **price certainty**.

In this section, we will explore the mechanisms traders use to tell the exchange exactly what they want. We will move beyond the simple concept of "buying" and "selling" to understand the difference between demanding a trade right now (Market Orders) and offering to trade at a specific price (Limit Orders). We will also see how auxiliary instructions—like how long an order should stay alive—act as the fine print in this digital contract.

The Fundamental Trade-off: Urgency vs. Thrift

Imagine you are standing in a chaotic bazaar. You want to buy a rare rug. You have two choices. You can walk up to a merchant and say, "I will take that rug right now, regardless of the price tag," or you can stand firmly in the middle of the aisle, hold up a sign that says "I will pay $500 for a rug," and wait for a merchant to agree to your terms.

The first approach guarantees you get the rug immediately, but you have no control over the final cost. The merchant sees your urgency and charges the full asking price. The second approach guarantees you will never pay more than $500, but you might stand there all day and go home empty-handed.

This is the central dilemma of market microstructure.

- **Market Orders** prioritize *execution certainty*. The trader is saying, "I need to trade now."
- **Limit Orders** prioritize *price certainty*. The trader is saying, "I need a specific price."

Every trade that occurs on an exchange is a marriage between these two types of participants: the impatient "taker" (Market Order) who consumes liquidity, and the patient "maker" (Limit Order) who provides it.

The Market Order: Paying for Immediacy

A **Market Order** is an instruction to buy or sell a security immediately at the best available price. It is the most aggressive instruction one can send to an exchange. When you click "Market Buy" on a brokerage app, you are essentially telling the matching engine: *"Find the lowest price anyone is willing to sell at, and pay it."*

It is crucial to understand that a Market Order does not guarantee a specific price. It guarantees a *fill*.

Crossing the Spread

Recall from the previous section that the "Spread" is the gap between the highest price a buyer is offering (Best Bid) and the lowest price a seller is accepting (Best Ask). A Market Order is the bridge that crosses that gap.

If you submit a Market Buy order, you are an *aggressor*. You cross the spread to hit the Best Ask. If the stock is quoted at $100.00 (Bid) / $100.05 (Ask), your Market Buy instantly executes at $100.05. You have paid the "spread cost" (5 cents) for the privilege of immediate ownership.

The Risk of Slippage

For small retail orders, the "best available price" is usually what you see on the screen. However, for large institutional orders, Market Orders carry a significant risk known as **slippage**.

Imagine there are 100 shares available at $100.05, and another 100 shares at $100.10. If a large mutual fund sends a Market Order to buy 200 shares, the engine will sweep the book. It will buy the first 100 shares at $100.05, exhaust that liquidity, and then immediately buy the next 100 shares at $100.10. The average price paid is higher than the displayed quote at the start of the trade. The order "slipped" upward because its sheer size consumed the available liquidity at the best price level.

The Limit Order: The Patience of the Maker

If the Market Order is the gas pedal, the **Limit Order** is the anchor. A Limit Order is an instruction to buy or sell a specific amount of stock at a specified price *or better*.

The phrase "or better" is key. A Limit Buy order at $50.00 sets a hard ceiling. The matching engine is programmed never to pay $50.01. However, if a seller suddenly appears offering the stock at $49.90, the engine will happily execute the Limit Buy at that lower price.

Resting Liquidity

Unlike Market Orders, which usually execute and vanish in microseconds, Limit Orders often do not trade immediately. If the stock is trading at $100.05 and you enter a Limit Buy at $99.50, your order does not cross the spread. It travels to the exchange and "rests" in the Order Book.

At that moment, you have become a **Liquidity Provider**. You have added a new "brick" to the wall of bids. Your order is now visible to the entire market (on a lit exchange), signaling to others that there is demand at $99.50. You are waiting for a seller to become impatient enough to send a Market Sell order that hits your price.

The Risk of Non-Execution

The danger of a Limit Order is not price (you control that), but *opportunity cost*. If the stock price rallies from $100.05 to $105.00, your Limit Buy at $99.50 will sit unfilled. You missed the trade completely because you were unwilling to cross the spread. In institutional trading, this is often called "chasing the market"—moving your limit price up repeatedly but never quite catching the rising price.

Marketable Limit Orders: A Hybrid Approach

There is a common hybrid used by professional algorithms called the **Marketable Limit Order**.

Suppose a trader wants to buy immediately (urgency), but refuses to pay a disastrous price if liquidity disappears (safety). They might see the Ask at $100.05 and send a Limit Buy order at $100.10.

Because the limit price ($100.10) is higher than the current best seller ($100.05), the matching engine treats this immediately as a trade. It executes against the $100.05 seller. However, if the price had spiked to $100.15 before the order arrived, a standard Market Order would have paid $100.15. The Marketable Limit Order, capped at $100.10, would stop, rest on the book, and refuse to overpay. It acts like a Market Order with an emergency brake.

Conditional Instructions: Time and Duration

Price and Quantity are the primary variables of an order, but "Time" is the third critical dimension. When a trader sends an order, they must specify how long that order remains valid. These instructions, known as *Time-in-Force* (TIF) modifiers, tell the matching engine when to give up.

Day vs. GTC

- **Day Orders:** This is the default setting for most manual trading. If the order is not executed by the time the market closes (e.g., 4:00 PM EST), the matching engine automatically cancels it. It wipes the slate clean for the next day.

- **GTC (Good 'Til Canceled):** These orders remain in the matching engine's memory indefinitely (or typically up to 60–90 days) until they are filled or the trader manually cancels them. Retail investors often use these to set "profit targets" far above the current price, waiting weeks for the market to reach them.

IOC: Immediate or Cancel

For High-Frequency Traders (HFT) and institutional algorithms, the most important time modifier is **IOC** (Immediate or Cancel).

An IOC order tells the matching engine: *"Execute as much of this order as you can right now, and immediately delete whatever you cannot fill."*

Why would a trader want this? Information leakage. Imagine an algorithm wants to buy 1,000 shares, but there are only 200 shares available at the best price.

- If the algorithm sends a standard Limit Order for 1,000 shares, it buys the 200 shares.

- The remaining 800 shares sit on the book as a resting Bid.

- Other participants see this new large Bid of 800 shares. They realize there is a big buyer present. They might front-run the order or pull their own sell orders, causing the price to rise.

By using an IOC, the algorithm buys the available 200 shares, and the remaining request for 800 shares vanishes instantly. The order leaves no footprint on the order book for competitors to analyze. The algorithm can then recalculate and try again milliseconds later.

Summary: The Code of Conduct

Ultimately, the matching engine is a logic gate that processes these instructions in a strict sequence. It looks at the **Type** (Market vs. Limit) to determine aggression. It looks at the **Price** to determine ranking. And it looks at the **Time-in-Force** to determine lifespan.

When you look at a scrolling ticker of stock prices, you are seeing the history of these collisions. Every trade printed is the result of a Market Order colliding with a Limit Order—impatience meeting patience.

1.4 Market Participants and Their Incentives

To a matching engine, the source of an order is irrelevant. The algorithm processes a binary instruction—buy or sell, price and quantity—without regard for who sent it. It does not care if the order comes from a grandmother investing her pension check, a massive sovereign wealth fund rebalancing a billion-dollar portfolio, or a computer server located in the basement of the exchange building. In the eyes of the engine, all incoming messages are equal.

However, to understand why markets move, why liquidity vanishes during crashes, or why spreads widen and narrow, we must look beyond the binary code and profile the humans (and algorithms) behind the orders. While their messages look identical, their motivations, time horizons, and constraints are radically different. The interaction between these disparate groups is what creates a functioning market. We can broadly categorize these participants into three distinct groups: the Retail Investor, the Institutional Investor, and the Market Maker.

The Retail Investor: The Long-Term Saver

The retail investor is likely the persona you are most familiar with—an individual trading their own capital. Retail participants typically trade in small sizes, often referred to as "odd lots" (amounts fewer than 100 shares).

Time Horizon: Long (Years or Decades).
Motivation: Capital appreciation, savings, or occasionally speculation.

Because retail investors trade infrequently and in small sizes, they are generally less sensitive to the minute-by-minute mechanics of the matching engine. When a retail investor sends a Market Order to buy 50 shares of a company, they are usually looking for immediate execution to secure a position they intend to hold for years. They are **price takers**, meaning they accept the current market price.

As discussed in the first section of this chapter, retail orders rarely reach the public "lit" exchanges (like the NYSE or Nasdaq) directly. Because their order flow is considered "uninformed"—meaning they likely do not possess secret news that will crash the stock price in the next millisecond—wholesalers maintain a high demand for these orders. Wholesalers prefer to trade against retail investors because the risk is low; the stock price is unlikely to move against the wholesaler immediately after the trade. Consequently, while the retail investor is the most numerous participant by headcount, they are the least visible to the central matching engine.

The Institutional Investor: The Moving Elephant

Institutional investors include pension funds, mutual funds, insurance companies, and university endowments. These entities manage vast pools of capital and trade in sizes that are difficult for the human mind to visualize. While a retail trader buys 50 shares, an institution might need to buy 5,000,000 shares.

Time Horizon: Medium to Long (Quarters to Years).
Motivation: Rebalancing portfolios, deploying assets, or hedging risk.

The primary problem for an institutional investor is simple physics: size creates displacement. If you drop a pebble into a bathtub (a retail order), the water level does not noticeably change. If you drop a boulder (an institutional order), the water is displaced violently.

If a mutual fund tries to buy 5 million shares using a simple Market Order, they would consume every available sell order in the book, driving the price up vertically. By the time they finished buying, the average price paid would be significantly higher than where the stock started. This phenomenon is called "market impact" or "slippage."

To avoid this, institutions must behave like submarines. They cannot show their hand. They utilize execution algorithms that slice their massive parent order into thousands of tiny child orders. They use the Limit Orders we defined previously to sit patiently in the order book, or they utilize Dark Pools (private exchanges) to find other institutions to trade with. Their relationship with the matching engine is adversarial: they need the engine's liquidity, but they must hide their intentions from it to preserve their capital.

The Market Maker and HFT: The Sprinters

The third group consists of Market Makers and High-Frequency Traders (HFT). Unlike the previous two groups, these participants have no interest in owning a piece of a company.

Time Horizon: Microseconds to Minutes.
Motivation: Earn the Bid-Ask Spread and rebates; maintain a **flat** position.

The market maker is a professional intermediary. Their business model is similar to a currency exchange booth at an airport. They stand ready to buy from anyone who wants to sell, and sell to anyone who wants to buy. Their goal is to buy at the Bid price and sell at the Ask price, pocketing the difference (the spread) as profit.

For a market maker, holding stock is a liability. If they buy shares from a seller, they immediately possess "inventory risk"—the risk that the market crashes while they are holding the stock. Therefore, they act with extreme urgency to offload that inventory to a buyer. This is the "Hot Potato" game of finance.

Because their profit per share is tiny (often fractions of a penny), they must trade massive volumes to survive. This necessitates speed. HFT firms co-locate their servers in the same data center as the exchange's matching engine to minimize the travel time of light through fiber optic cables.

The Ecosystem of Incentives

The matching engine functions effectively only because these three groups have opposing needs that complement one another. This is the "Symbiosis of Time Horizons."

Consider a typical trade lifecycle:

- **Pension Fund (Institution)** needs to sell a massive amount of stock. It cannot dump it all at once, so it places a Limit Order to sell above the current price. It provides **patience**.
- **HFT algorithm (Market Maker)** detects an imbalance. It buys a small chunk of that stock, taking on the risk, betting it can flip it quickly. It provides **immediacy**.
- **Retail Investor** logs in to buy stock for their retirement. They send a Market Order. The wholesaler or exchange matches them against the HFT's inventory.

In this transaction, the Institution got to sell a large size without crashing the price. The Retail investor got their stock instantly. The Market Maker earned a tiny spread for bridging the time gap between the Institution's sell order and the Retailer's buy order.

If everyone were a long-term investor, trading would grind to a halt because everyone would be holding. If everyone were a high-frequency trader, volatility would explode as algorithms passed the hot potato back and forth with no final destination. The matching engine is the arena where these conflicting time horizons—years, days, and microseconds—collide and resolve into a single price.

Chapter 2

Inside the Machine: The Matching Engine

If the stock market were a physical auction house, it would be chaos. Instead, modern finance relies on a silent, relentless piece of software: the Matching Engine. In this chapter, we strip away the screens and charts to look directly at the digital logic that governs billions of dollars in milliseconds. We will trace the precise millisecond-by-millisecond journey of an order-from the moment it leaves your computer to the instant it collides with a counterparty-demystifying the strict rules of queueing, priority, and execution that determine the winners and losers of every trade.

2.1 The Order Lifecycle

When a trader sits at their desk and clicks "Buy," the screen often blinks a confirmation in a fraction of a second. To the human eye, the action feels instantaneous, as if the trade happened locally on the computer. In reality, that click initiates a high-speed journey through a complex industrial pipeline. The order does not simply teleport into the market; it must travel physically across cables, pass through strict security checkpoints, stand in line, and finally be processed by the core logic of the exchange.

To understand the matching engine, we must first understand the pipeline that feeds it. An exchange is not a cloud of vague interactions; it is a rigid, linear factory floor. Every instruction is processed in a specific sequence, ensuring that the market remains deterministic–meaning that if we were to replay all the day's inputs in the exact same order, we would get the exact same result. This predictability is the bedrock of market fairness.

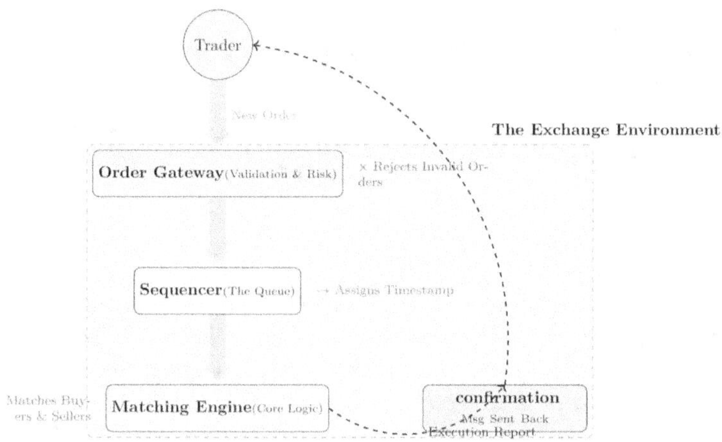

The Gateway: The Bouncer

The first stop for any order is the **Order Entry Gateway**. Before an order can interact with other traders, it must prove it belongs there. You can think of the Gateway as the "bouncer" of the exchange. It stands strictly outside the matching engine and performs a series of rapid validation checks.

First, it checks **syntax**: Is the order message formatted correctly? Does it speak the exchange's language (typically a protocol called FIX or a proprietary binary protocol)? If the computer is speaking gibberish, the Gateway rejects it immediately.

Second, and more importantly, it checks **risk and validity**. Does the trader actually have permission to trade this stock? Is the account currently suspended? Is the order size surprisingly large–perhaps a "fat finger" error where a trader meant to buy 100 shares but accidentally typed 100,000?

If an order fails any of these tests, it is bounced immediately. It never reaches the matching engine, and as far as the market is concerned, the order never existed. Only "clean" orders are allowed to pass through the velvet rope to the next stage.

The Sequencer: Taking a Number

Once an order passes the Gateway, it enters a critical phase known as **sequencing**. In modern electronic markets, fairness is defined by time. If you and I both want to buy Apple stock at the same price, the person who arrived first should get served first.

However, orders arrive from all over the world via different cables. To establish absolute truth, the exchange passes every valid order through a Sequencer. Imagine a deli counter where everyone must take a ticket number. The Sequencer assigns a precise timestamp and a sequence number to the order.

From this moment on, the order's place in history is fixed. It joins a single-file line (a queue). Even if the exchange is processing millions of trades, the core engine usually handles them one by one, in strict numerical order. This prevents "race conditions," where two orders might try to claim the same stock simultaneously. In the engine, there is no "simultaneously"–there is only before and after.

The Core Engine and Acknowledgement

Finally, the order reaches the **Matching Engine** itself. This is the brain of the operation. The engine takes the order off the conveyor belt and compares it against the "book" of existing buy and sell offers. (We will explore the structure of this book in the next section).

Depending on the state of the market, the engine will do one of two things:

- **Match:** If there is a counter-party willing to trade at that price, a trade is generated.
- **Rest:** If there is no immediate match, the order is placed into the book to wait for a future seller.

Crucially, the lifecycle isn't complete until the trader knows the result. The engine fires off an **Acknowledgement** (or "Ack") message. This confirmation travels back out through the gateway, across the wire, and lights up the trader's screen. While this entire loop–from the trader's computer, through the gateway, sequencer, engine, and back–might involve crossing miles of fiber optic cable and passing through multiple servers, modern exchanges complete the cycle in microseconds (millionths of a second).

2.2 The Limit Order Book

Once an order survives the scrutiny of the Gateway, having passed validation, risk checks, and credit limits, it arrives at the core of the exchange: the Matching Engine. Here, the order enters a strict, deterministic world defined by a single data structure known as the **Limit Order Book** (LOB).

If the Gateway is the bouncer, the Limit Order Book is the dance floor. It is the organized record of exactly who wants to buy, who wants to sell, at what price, and in what quantity. Understanding the anatomy of the LOB is essential because, in modern electronic trading, the market *is* the limit order book.

The Anatomy of the Book

At its simplest, the Limit Order Book consists of two lists facing each other: the **Bids** and the **Asks** (also called Offers).

- **The Bids (Buyers):** This list contains all the traders looking to buy the asset. Buyers naturally want to pay the lowest possible price. However, to get their order filled, they must compete with other buyers. Therefore, the Bids are sorted by price from highest to lowest. The buyer willing to pay the most sits at the very top of the list; this is known as the "Best Bid."

- **The Asks (Sellers):** This list contains all the traders looking to sell the asset. Sellers want to receive the highest possible price. To compete, they must lower their asking price. Consequently, the Asks are sorted from lowest to highest. The seller willing to accept the least amount of money sits at the bottom of this list; this is the "Best Ask."

These two lists are typically visualized as a vertical ladder. Prices increase as you move up the ladder. The Bids sit on the lower rungs (the "green" side), and the Asks sit on the upper rungs (the "red" side).

The Spread

In a typical resting state, the highest price a buyer is willing to pay (e.g., $100.00) is lower than the lowest price a seller is willing to accept (e.g., $100.01). If a buyer were willing to pay $100.01, a trade would happen immediately, and the order would not "rest" in the book.

The gap between the Best Bid and the Best Ask is called the **Bid-Ask Spread**. This gap represents the "no-man's-land" where no liquidity exists. The width of the spread is a key indicator of a market's efficiency and liquidity. In highly liquid stocks like Apple or Microsoft, the spread is usually a single penny (the minimum price variation). In illiquid stocks, the spread might be ten or twenty cents, representing a much higher cost to cross the gap and execute a trade immediately.

Price Levels and Queues

A common misconception is that a "quote" on the screen represents a single person. When you see a bid for 1,000 shares at $100.00, it is rarely a single trader. Instead, the Limit Order Book aggregates interest at distinct **Price Levels**.

Think of every valid price point (e.g., $100.00, $100.01, $100.02) as a bucket. When an order arrives at $100.00, it doesn't just sit on a list; it joins a queue specific to that price level. If five different banks all submit buy orders for 200 shares at $100.00, the matching engine aggregates them. The public data feed broadcasts: "Price: $100.00, Size: 1,000."

The internal reality, however, is a sequence of individual orders lined up behind one another. This "depth" at a specific price level is crucial for traders who need to move large sizes. A price level with only 100 shares is "thin," while a price level with 50,000 shares offers a "thick" layer of protection or resistance.

The following chart illustrates the vertical structure of the book, showing how Bids and Asks stack up, separated by the spread, and introducing the concept of hidden depth.

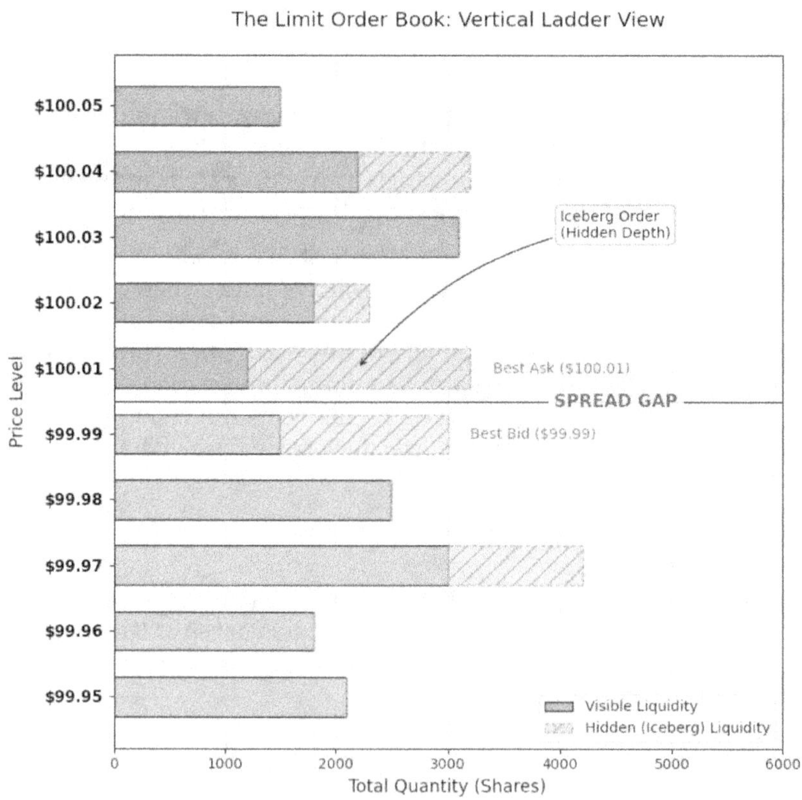

Iceberg Orders: The Visible and the Invisible

As depicted in the ladder chart above, the Limit Order Book contains more than meets the eye. Notice the hatched sections extending beyond the solid colored bars. These represent **Iceberg Orders** (also known as Reserve Orders).

Institutional traders often need to buy or sell quantities that are significantly larger than the average size displayed in the book. If a mutual fund placed a single order to sell 100,000 shares at $100.01, the sheer size of the order would panic the market. Buyers would disappear (canceling their bids), and the price would likely crash before the mutual fund could sell its shares. This phenomenon is known as "market impact."

To minimize market impact, exchanges offer Iceberg orders. These orders allow a trader to submit a large total quantity (e.g., 100,000 shares) while instructing the matching engine to only display a small fraction of it (e.g., 1,000 shares) to the public.

To the outside world, the book looks standard: "1,000 shares for sale at $100.01." When a buyer purchases those 1,000 shares, the engine instantly "reloads" the order from the hidden reserve, displaying another 1,000 shares at the same price. This cycle continues until the entire hidden quantity is exhausted.

In the Limit Order Book's memory, the order exists as a single entity, but logically it is treated as two distinct parts: the **Displayed Quantity** and the **Reserve Quantity**. The Displayed Quantity sits in the visible queue, interacting with the market. The Reserve Quantity waits in the background, invisible to other traders, ready to replenish the visible tip of the iceberg.

By structuring the market as a series of price levels, queues, and hidden reserves, the Limit Order Book serves as the complex staging ground for the most critical event in the exchange: the match. However, knowing where the orders sit is only half the battle. When multiple traders all want to buy at the same price, the engine must decide who gets served first. This necessitates a strict set of rules known as Priority Logic, which we will explore in the next section.

2.3 Priority Rules: Who Goes First?

In the previous section, we visualized the Limit Order Book as a set of lists: a list of buyers organized by price, and a list of sellers organized by price. However, these lists are rarely static, single-line entries. In a popular stock like Apple or Microsoft, there might be hundreds of different traders all willing to buy shares at the exact same price.

If there are five thousand shares available to be bought at $150.00, but a seller only sends in an order to sell one hundred shares, who gets them? Does the exchange split the shares equally? Does it favor the largest bank? Does it favor the order that has been waiting the longest?

To solve this problem of scarcity, matching engines rely on a strict set of algorithms known as **priority rules**. While there are exotic variations in some specific markets, the vast majority of stock exchanges globally operate on a standard known as **Price-Time Priority**.

You can think of this algorithm as a two-step filter used to sort the chaotic influx of orders into a disciplined line.

The First Rule: Price Priority

The first rule is the most intuitive: **Price is King**.

The primary goal of an exchange is to facilitate trade at the best possible terms. Therefore, the matching engine always gives priority to the most aggressive prices.

- If you are a **buyer**, a higher bid ($150.05) is always ranked ahead of a lower bid ($150.00).
- If you are a **seller**, a lower offer ($150.10) is always ranked ahead of a higher offer ($150.15).

This rule creates a competitive auction. If a trader really wants to ensure their order is executed, they can "jump the queue" simply by improving their price. If there is a long line of people waiting to buy at $150.00, and you enter a buy order at $150.01, the matching engine immediately places you in front of every single trader at the $150.00 level. You are now at the "top of the book."

The Second Rule: Time Priority

The situation becomes more complex and more technically critical when multiple traders offer the exact same price. In modern electronic markets, this happens constantly. At any given second, there may be dozens of hedge funds, banks, and retail investors all bidding $150.00.

Since the price is identical, the engine cannot use the first rule to decide who goes first. It moves to the tiebreaker: **Time Priority**.

This works exactly like a line at a supermarket checkout or a movie theater. It follows a principle engineers call **FIFO** (First-In, First-Out).

1. **Arrival matters:** The engine stamps every valid order with a precise arrival time (often down to the nanosecond).
2. **The Queue:** If Trader A's order arrives at 10:00:00.001 and Trader B's order arrives at 10:00:00.002, Trader A is placed ahead of Trader B.
3. **No cutting allowed:** Even if Trader B is a massive global bank wanting to buy 1,000,000 shares, and Trader A is an individual buying 10 shares, Trader A gets filled first because they arrived first.

This creates a physical queue at every single price level. If you look at a limit order book, the "quantity" shown at a price of $150.00 is actually the aggregate total of a long line of individual orders, stacked one behind the other based on when they arrived at the engine.

The Fairness of the Machine

It is difficult to overstate how important this strict serial processing is for market integrity. In the physical trading pits of the past, a loud voice or a personal relationship with a broker might have helped you get a trade done before someone else. In the electronic matching engine, those factors do not exist.

The engine is deterministic. It does not know who owns the order; it only knows the numbers. It asks two questions in sequence:

1. Who is offering the best price?
2. Among those offering the best price, who arrived first?

This creates a powerful incentive structure. To get your trade executed, you must either pay a better price (benefiting the person on the other side of the trade) or you must commit your capital earlier than your competitors (taking on the risk of waiting). This structure keeps the market moving and rewards those who provide liquidity to the system early.

If you are at the back of the queue at a specific price level, the only way you will get shares is if the seller has enough stock to satisfy everyone ahead of you in line. If the seller's order runs out of shares before it reaches your position in the queue, you get nothing. You remain in the book, waiting for the next seller to arrive.

2.4 Matching Logic and Determinism

Up to this point, we have viewed the matching engine as a storage facility—a highly organized warehouse where orders are checked at the door (the Gateway), sorted by price, and queued by time (the Limit Order Book). However, a storage facility is static. The market exists to facilitate exchange. This section examines the dynamic moment when a trade actually occurs: the precise instant an incoming order collides with a resting order.

In industry terms, this is the distinction between **Maker** and **Taker**. The resting orders sitting in the queue are the **Makers**; they make the market by providing liquidity and waiting for a partner. The incoming order that triggers a trade is the **Taker**; it takes liquidity off the table by accepting a price that is currently available.

The Collision Point

A match occurs strictly when the price of an incoming buy order overlaps with the price of a resting sell order (or vice versa). This is often referred to as "crossing the spread."

Imagine the current market for a stock looks like this:

- **Lowest Sell Offer (Ask):** $100.00
- **Highest Buy Bid:** $99.95

The gap between $99.95 and $100.00 is the spread. If a trader enters a buy order at $99.98, no trade occurs. The order simply joins the queue on the bid side, narrowing the spread. However, if a trader enters a buy order with a limit of $100.00 (or higher), the engine detects an overlap. The "potential energy" of the resting sell order is converted into the "kinetic energy" of a trade.

The Golden Rule of Execution Price

A common misconception among new traders concerns the price at which the trade is executed. If a seller is asking $100.00, and you panic and submit a limit buy order for $105.00 to ensure you get the stock, do you pay $105.00?

The answer is no. You pay $100.00.

The matching engine operates on a principle that favors the resting order. The price of the trade is always determined by the **limit price of the maker (the resting order)**, not the taker. When your $105.00 bid hits the engine, the logic checks for available shares. It finds shares available at $100.00. Since $100.00 is within your acceptable limit (it is better than $105.00), the engine executes the trade at the best available price. This mechanism protects aggressive traders from overpaying significantly when liquidity is available at better rates.

Sweeping the Book

Markets are rarely satisfied by a single order. Often, an institutional investor needs to buy more shares than are available at the single best price. This leads to a process known as "sweeping" or "walking" the book.

Consider a scenario where an aggressive buyer wants 1,000 shares. The sell side of the order book looks like this:

- **Level 1:** 200 shares @ $100.00
- **Level 2:** 300 shares @ $100.01
- **Level 3:** 1,000 shares @ $100.05

If the buyer sends a “Market Order” (an instruction to buy immediately at any price) for 1,000 shares, the engine processes the trade sequentially:

- It consumes the entire Level 1 (200 shares) at $100.00.
- The buyer still needs 800 shares. The engine moves up to Level 2 and consumes all 300 shares at $100.01.
- The buyer still needs 500 shares. The engine moves to Level 3, consuming 500 of the available 1,000 shares at $100.05.

The buyer has now “swept” three levels of the book. While the trade happened instantaneously from the trader’s perspective, the engine performed three distinct calculations. Crucially, the buyer does not get a single price; they get a **Volume Weighted Average Price (VWAP)**. In this case, the average price is slightly higher than the starting price of $100.00. This increase in cost caused by the order’s own size is called “market impact” or “slippage.”

Determinism: The Absence of Randomness

Finally, it is vital to understand that the matching engine is a deterministic state machine. This means there is absolutely no randomness in how a match is calculated. If you were to replay the exact same sequence of orders (inputs) into the engine ten times, you would get the exact same trade log (outputs) ten times.

Every instruction is processed one by one. The engine does not “choose” who gets filled based on fairness or estimation; it follows rigid logic:

- Check if the incoming price crosses the best resting price.
- If yes, calculate the quantity that can be filled.

- Generate the trade report.
- If the incoming order still has quantity left, repeat the process with the next price level.
- Once the incoming order is filled or runs out of matching prices, place any remainder in the book as a new resting order.

This determinism is the bedrock of trust in financial markets. It ensures that despite the chaos of millions of messages per second, the outcome for every participant is mathematically predictable based on the rules of Price and Time priority.

2.5 Managing State: Cancels and Modifications

In the previous sections, we treated orders as if they were set in stone: a trader sends an order, and it sits in the book until it is either executed or canceled. In reality, the market is fluid. Valuations change in milliseconds, and traders frequently need to adjust their resting limit orders to reflect new information. They might want to change the price to be more competitive or increase the size of their order to capture more liquidity.

To the trader, this feels like a simple update-a quick edit to an existing instruction. However, to the matching engine, managing these changes requires a strict set of rules to preserve the fairness of the Price-Time Priority queue. The mechanism used for this is often called a **Cancel/Replace** message.

The Cost of Changing Your Mind

When a modification request reaches the matching engine, the system must decide whether the order gets to keep its place in line or if it must go to the back of the queue. This decision is critical because, as we have established, queue position is valuable. Being at the front means you get filled first; being at the back means you might miss the trade entirely.

The engine applies a logic that can be likened to strict etiquette in a supermarket checkout line.

- **Reducing Size (The "No Penalty" Rule):** Imagine you are standing in line at the checkout with ten items. While waiting, you decide you only want to buy seven of them. You place three items on a nearby shelf. Does this hurt the people behind you? No. In fact, it speeds up the line.

  Similarly, if a trader modifies an order to *decrease* its quantity (e.g., reducing a buy order from 1,000 shares to 500 shares), the matching engine typically allows the order to retain its original timestamp. The order stays in its current position in the queue, simply with a smaller size.

- **Increasing Size (The "Back of the Line" Rule):** Now imagine you are in that same line, but your friend runs up with a cart full of twenty extra items and tries to add them to your pile. If the cashier allowed this, the customers behind you would be rightfully angry. You are significantly altering the wait time for everyone else.

  To prevent this unfairness, if a trader modifies an order to *increase* its quantity, the matching engine treats it as a new order. The original order is canceled, and a new order for the larger amount is added to the very end of the queue at that price level. The trader loses their priority.

- **Changing Price:** Changing the price is effectively removing your interest from one price level and inserting it into another. If you move your buy order from $100.00 to $100.01, you are leaving the $100.00 queue entirely and joining the $100.01 queue. Regardless of whether you are moving the price up or down, a price change always results in a new timestamp. You are entering a new line, so you must start at the back.

The Atomic Swap

From a technical perspective, a "modify" message is an atomic operation-meaning it happens all at once or not at all. The engine effectively performs a "Cancel" of the old ID and a "New Order" entry for the new parameters in a single, indivisible step.

This atomicity is crucial for risk management. If a trader had to manually send a cancel message, wait for confirmation, and then send a new order message, there would be a brief window of time where they had zero orders in the market (leaving them unhedged) or a window where both orders might exist (accidentally doubling their position). The Cancel/Replace functionality ensures that the transition is seamless, protecting the trader from these "race conditions" while strictly enforcing the priority rules that keep the market fair for everyone else.

Chapter 3

Auctions and Price Discovery

Every trading day begins and ends not with a high-speed race, but with a calculated pause. While continuous trading dominates the headlines with its microsecond speeds, the market's most critical benchmarks-the Opening and Closing prices-are determined through a completely different mechanism. This chapter lifts the lid on the auction process, revealing how exchanges stop the clock to aggregate orders, maximize liquidity, and discover a single fair price that satisfies the crowd.

3.1 Continuous Matching vs. Batch Auctions

When we imagine the stock market, we typically visualize a ticker tape scrolling across a screen or a price chart that wiggles up and down, second by second. This constant movement represents the market's standard operating mode, known as **continuous trading**. In this mode, the matching engine operates like a high-speed revolving door. Orders arrive, check the room for an immediate match, and either execute or wait in line. It is a serial process: first come, first served.

In a continuous market, speed is the defining factor. If you want to buy 100 shares of Microsoft, you enter the "revolving door." If a seller is already there waiting, the trade happens instantly. If you are a millisecond faster than another buyer, you get the stock, and they do not. This system works brilliantly for most of the trading day, facilitating the smooth flow of liquidity.

However, there are moments when the revolving door cannot handle the traffic. Consider the market open at 9:30 AM. Overnight news has accumulated, earnings reports have been released, and global events have shifted investor sentiment. If the exchange opened the doors for continuous trading immediately, thousands of buy and sell orders would try to jam through the door simultaneously. The result would be chaotic volatility: the first trade might occur at $100, the next at $105, and the third back down at $101, all within a fraction of a second, depending purely on who arrived first.

To solve this, exchanges utilize a completely different mechanism called a **batch auction** (often referred to simply as a "call auction" or "cross").

If continuous trading is a revolving door, a batch auction is a **floodgate** or a lock in a canal. During an auction period, the market does not match orders immediately. Instead, the matching engine effectively puts up a "Stop" sign. It allows buyers and sellers to line up, but it prevents them from interacting.

During this pause, the engine accumulates all interest into a pool. It accepts buy orders and sell orders, stacking them up to see the full picture of supply and demand. The goal is not to trade as fast as possible, but to find a single price that satisfies the maximum number of participants.

Once the auction period ends (for example, at the exact moment of the market open), the engine removes the barrier. It processes the entire batch of accumulated orders in a single mathematical operation. Instead of a stream of trades occurring at different prices based on arrival time, the auction creates a massive "print" where thousands of shares change hands at one single, consensus price.

This distinction is vital for understanding how markets discover price. Continuous matching discovers price incrementally, trade by trade. It is efficient for maintaining flow. Auctions, conversely, discover price by aggregation. They are necessary at specific moments-such as the open, the close, or after a volatility halt-to gather scattered liquidity and establish a solid equilibrium price before the revolving door starts spinning again.

3.2 The Opening and Closing Cross

If continuous trading is the steady hum of the engine, the Opening and Closing Crosses are the ignition spark and the parking brake. These two events are the single most significant liquidity moments of the trading day. They are not merely the first and last trades; they are distinct mechanisms designed to consolidate a massive amount of interest into a single, robust price.

To understand why these specific auctions matter, consider the concept of an "official" price. When you look up a stock's performance for the day, or when a mutual fund calculates the value of its portfolio, they do not use a random trade that occurred at 11:42 AM. They use the *Closing Price.* Because billions of dollars in derivatives, index funds, and institutional portfolios are benchmarked to this specific number, the market cannot rely on the serendipity of continuous matching to set it. It requires a formal gathering of buyers and sellers—a batch auction—to ensure the price is representative of true market sentiment.

This process is known as "The Cross." While the Opening Cross (typically at 9:30 AM ET) sets the baseline for the day, the Closing Cross (4:00 PM ET) is often the busiest fraction of a second in the entire trading session.

Auction-Specific Instructions

In the continuous market, you place a Limit Order or a Market Order, and the matching engine tries to execute it immediately. However, for the Open and Close, traders use specific order types that function like reservations for a future event.

The two most common instructions are:

- **Market-On-Close (MOC):** This is an instruction to the exchange that says, "I need to buy 1,000 shares, and I simply must be part of the final print. I do not care what the price is; just ensure I am included in the Closing Cross." These orders are guaranteed to execute (provided there is liquidity), but the trader surrenders control over the price.

- **Limit-On-Close (LOC):** This adds a price constraint. The trader says, "I want to participate in the Closing Cross, but only if the final price is $150.00 or lower." If the auction creates a price of $150.01, this order will be left behind.

These orders sit in a separate "bucket" within the matching engine, unseen by the continuous market, waiting for the auction trigger.

The Timeline and the "Lock-In"

An auction is not instantaneous; it is a process with a strict timeline. If the exchange allowed traders to enter and cancel auction orders right up until the final millisecond, it would create chaos. High-frequency traders could fake interest to push the predicted price up or down, only to cancel their orders at the last second—a practice known as "spoofing."

To prevent this, exchanges enforce a **Lock-In Period** or "Cutoff."

Let us look at the standard Closing Cross timeline. Throughout the day, traders can enter MOC and LOC orders freely. However, at a specific time (usually 3:50 PM or 3:55 PM, depending on the exchange), the window narrows.

- **Pre-Cutoff:** Traders can enter, modify, or cancel auction orders without restriction. The matching engine quietly tallies the buy and sell interest.

- **The Cutoff (Lock-In):** Once the clock strikes the cutoff time, the rules tighten. You generally cannot cancel an existing auction order. You are committed. If you put in an order to sell 50,000 shares On-Close, the market is now counting on that supply.

- **Imbalance Publication:** After the cutoff, the exchange begins broadcasting "Imbalance Messages." The engine compares all the accumulated buy orders to all the accumulated sell orders. If there are 1,000,000 shares to buy but only 800,000 shares to sell, the exchange publishes a "Buy Imbalance" of 200,000 shares.

This broadcast acts as a flare signal to the market. It tells sophisticated traders: "We are short 200,000 shares for the auction. If you have shares to sell, bring them now!" This attracts new liquidity to balance the scales before the final bell.

At exactly 4:00 PM, the gate drops. The continuous market halts, and the matching engine takes all the locked-in auction orders (MOC/LOC) and combines them with eligible orders from the regular book. It runs the pricing algorithm—which we will detail in the next section—and executes all matched trades at a single price.

This transition from the fluid, cancel-anytime nature of continuous trading to the rigid, committed structure of the Cross is essential. It sacrifices flexibility for stability, ensuring that the price widely quoted as "the value of the company" is derived from the maximum possible agreement between buyers and sellers.

3.3 Solving for the Price

If the continuous market is a stream of individual interactions-one buyer meeting one seller-the auction is a collective negotiation. By the time the Opening or Closing Cross arrives, the exchange has accumulated a massive "batch" of orders. There are thousands of buy orders willing to pay different amounts and thousands of sell orders asking for different prices.

But an auction cannot output a range of prices. It must produce exactly *one* price: the Clearing Price. All buy orders eligible to trade at that price will be filled, and all sell orders eligible at that price will be matched against them.

How does the matching engine select that single magic number from the chaos of thousands of conflicting desires? It does not use complex differential calculus or predictive AI. Instead, it uses a brute-force approach based on a simple, utilitarian rule: **Maximum Executable Volume**.

The engine's goal is to find the price point that allows the highest number of shares to trade hands.

The "What-If" Game

To find this price, the matching engine runs a rapid series of simulations. It looks at every price level where an order exists and asks, "What if we set the price here?"

Imagine a simplified scenario for a stock, say "TechCorp."

- **Scenario A: A Low Price ($100).** At this low price, buyers are thrilled. Everyone who wanted to buy at $100, $101, or $105 is happy to pay $100. Demand is huge. However, sellers are stingy; only those willing to sell for $100 or less will participate. High-priced sellers walk away. Because you need a seller for every buyer, the total volume is limited by the scarcity of sellers.
- **Scenario B: A High Price ($110).** Now the tables turn. Sellers are ecstatic; everyone asking $100, $105, or $110 is ready to sell. But buyers balk. Only the most aggressive buyers remain. The total volume is now limited by the scarcity of buyers.
- **Scenario C: The "Goldilocks" Price ($105).** At this middle ground, the engine finds the sweet spot. The price is high enough to entice a substantial number of sellers, but low enough to retain a substantial number of buyers.

The engine compares the "matched volume" at $100, $110, and $105 (and every penny in between). The price level that results in the biggest pile of traded shares wins. It is a democratic process weighted by conviction: the price that satisfies the most volume becomes the official Opening or Closing price.

The chart illustrates this "crossover" point. The downward slope represents buyers (who buy more as prices drop), and the upward slope represents sellers (who sell more as prices rise). The peak of activity occurs exactly where they intersect.

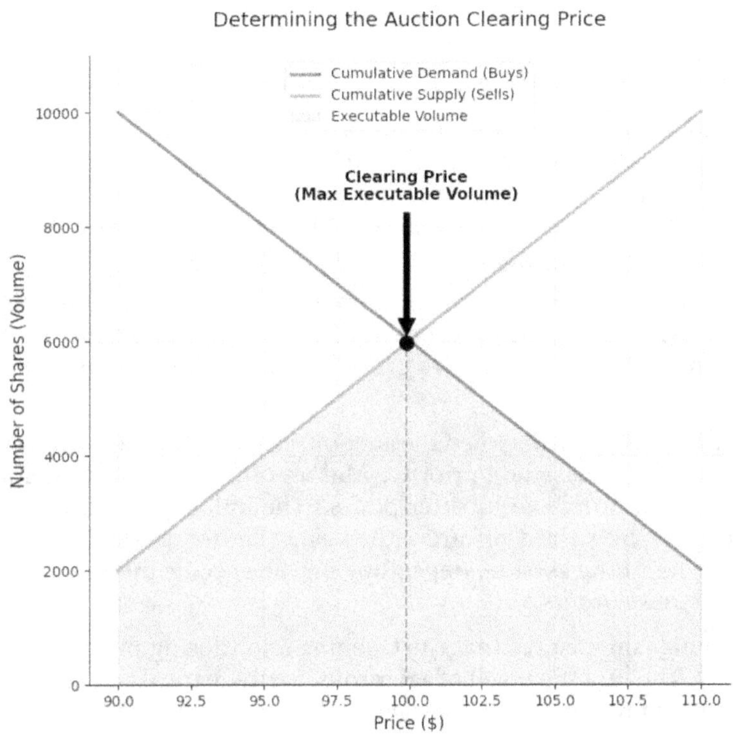

Resolving Imbalances

In a perfect world, supply and demand would meet exactly-100,000 shares for sale and 100,000 shares wanted at the clearing price. In the real world, this essentially never happens. Even at the optimal "Goldilocks" price, there is usually a mismatch.

Let us say the auction algorithm determines the clearing price is $50.00.

- **Total Buy Interest at $50:** 150,000 shares.
- **Total Sell Interest at $50:** 100,000 shares.

The exchange can only match what is available. In this case, 100,000 shares will trade. This is the "matched volume." But what happens to the extra 50,000 shares that buyers wanted?

This leftover quantity is called the **Imbalance**.

Throughout the minutes leading up to the auction (during the "lock-in" period mentioned earlier), the exchange broadcasts this data to the public. Feeds will flash messages like: *"Buy Imbalance: 50,000 shares."* This is a signal to the market: "We have too many buyers; we need more sellers to step in, or the price will have to jump higher."

High-frequency traders and institutional desks monitor these imbalance messages closely. If they see a Buy Imbalance, they might rush to send in "Sell On Close" orders to fill that gap, hoping to capture the liquidity.

If the imbalance remains when the auction executes, the algorithm processes the orders based on priority. Market orders get filled first, followed by limit orders with better prices. The unlucky 50,000 shares that couldn't be paired off are either cancelled or pushed into the continuous trading session, depending on the specific instructions attached to those orders.

This mechanism ensures that the Opening and Closing prices are not arbitrary. They are the result of a rigorous, mathematical contest to satisfy the maximum number of participants, turning a fragmented pile of orders into a single, definitive moment of market consensus.

3.4 Volatility Controls and Halts

So far, we have viewed the auction primarily as a tool for starting and ending the trading day-a bookend for the open and the close. However, the matching engine also keeps the auction logic in its back pocket as an emergency brake. This creates a critical safety mechanism known as the **volatility halt**.

In the continuous market, speed is the dominant factor. As we discussed earlier, the "first-come, first-served" nature of the continuous order book is efficient when prices move incrementally. But what happens when a stock price falls off a cliff? If a company announces catastrophic news, or if a computer algorithm malfunctions and sends a flood of erroneous sell orders, the price can plummet vertically in milliseconds.

In these moments of panic, the speed of the continuous market becomes a liability. Liquidity evaporates, spreads widen to ridiculous levels, and trades execute at prices that bear no relation to the asset's true value. To prevent the market from eating itself, the exchange's matching engine is programmed to recognize these anomalies and intervene.

Limit Up-Limit Down (LULD)

The primary mechanism for this intervention is a protocol known as **Limit Up-Limit Down (LULD)**. While the specific percentages can vary based on the tier of the stock and the time of day, the concept is intuitive. Imagine a "band" or a safe zone that floats around the current stock price. If the stock is trading at $100, the exchange might enforce a band between $95 (Limit Down) and $105 (Limit Up).

As the price moves gradually, the bands move with it. However, if a sudden surge of aggressive buy or sell orders hits the book and tries to push the price outside these bands immediately, the matching engine refuses to execute those trades. It puts the stock into a "Limit State." If the buying or selling pressure persists for 15 seconds without resolving, the engine makes a decisive switch: it triggers a **Trading Halt**.

The Pause That Refreshes

When a halt is triggered, the matching engine effectively flips a switch from "Continuous Trading Mode" to "Auction Mode." This is the key insight: a trading halt is not simply a stoppage; it is a transition to an intraday auction.

During a five-minute volatility halt, the following occurs inside the engine:

- **Execution Stops:** No trades are allowed to occur. The ticker tape stops moving.
- **Order Entry Continues:** Just like in the pre-market Opening

Cross, market participants can send new orders, cancel old ones, or adjust their limit prices.

- **Information Aggregation:** The market uses this time to digest the news. Humans step in to override algorithms. Market makers assess the imbalance.

This pause allows the "fog of war" to lift. In a continuous market, a flash crash happens faster than human reaction time. By halting the stock, the exchange forces a timeout, allowing rational buyers to enter the market and provide support.

The Re-opening Auction

Once the five-minute halt expires, the market does not simply resume continuous trading where it left off. If it did, the panic might instantly resume. Instead, the engine runs the exact same algorithm described in the previous section ("Solving for the Price").

The engine calculates the supply and demand curves based on the orders accumulated during the halt. It looks for the single price point where the maximum volume can be traded-the **maximizing price**.

This process leads to a "re-opening print." A single bulk trade occurs, clearing out the imbalance and establishing a new, valid consensus price. Only after this auction is complete does the engine revert to continuous, serial matching.

In this way, the auction serves as a stabilizing force. If continuous trading is like a rushing river that can occasionally flood, the volatility auction is the floodgate that closes to control the water level, ensuring that when the flow resumes, it does so safely and predictably.

Chapter 4

The View from Outside: Data, Latency, and Visibility

For most observers, the market appears on a screen as a flickering grid of numbers-limitless, immediate, and precise. But this view is an illusion created by digital signals that have traveled a long, jagged path. This chapter steps outside the matching engine to explore the imperfect window through which the world watches it work. We will uncover why the price you see is always slightly in the past, why the official 'tape' doesn't always match the quotes, and why the queue you join is often far more dangerous than it looks.

4.1 Market Data Feeds: Depth and Top-of-Book

To the uninitiated observer, the stock market appears to be a single, fluid stream of numbers—tickers scrolling across the bottom of a television screen or green and red flashes on a smartphone app. However, what most casual observers see is not the market itself, but a highly summarized report of the market.

Understanding how a matching engine works requires us to first understand the "inputs" that traders see. Before a trader can decide to buy or sell, they must know the price. But "the price" is not a singular fact; it is a layered landscape of information. Exchanges do not treat data as a mere byproduct of trading; they treat it as a product to be packaged and sold. The more you pay, the more you see.

This hierarchy of visibility creates two distinct experiences of the market: the "Top-of-Book" view available to retail investors, and the "Depth-of-Book" view utilized by professionals.

Level 1: The Keyhole View

When you check a stock price on a free website or a standard brokerage app, you are looking at **Level 1** data. In industry terms, this is often called the "Top-of-Book" or the "Best Bid and Offer" (BBO).

The matching engine constantly sorts thousands of buy and sell orders. Level 1 data takes this complex sorting process and filters it down to exactly two numbers:

- **The Best Bid:** The highest price anyone is currently willing to pay to buy the stock.
- **The Best Offer (Ask):** The lowest price anyone is currently willing to accept to sell the stock.

If the best bid is $100.00 and the best offer is $100.05, that is all you see. You do not see how many shares are available at those prices, nor do you see the thousands of other orders waiting slightly further away—for example, a buyer willing to pay $99.99 or a seller asking for $100.06.

Trading with Level 1 data is analogous to looking through a keyhole into a room. You can see the person standing directly in front of the door (the best price), but you have no idea how crowded the room is behind them. You cannot see if there is a massive line of buyers forming just inches out of view, or if the room is virtually empty.

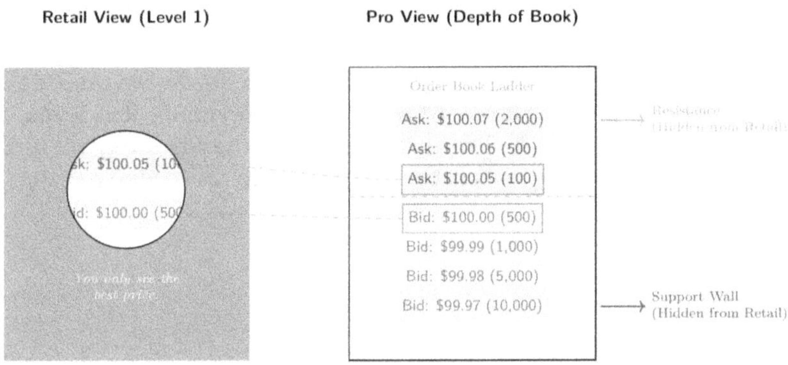

Level 2 and 3: Opening the Door

Professional traders, algorithms, and market makers subscribe to **Level 2** or **Level 3** data feeds (often called "Depth-of-Book"). These feeds strip away the filter. Instead of seeing only the winner of the auction (the best price), the trader sees the entire list of participants.

This data is visualized as a "ladder" or vertical list of prices.

- **The Ask Ladder:** Above the current price, you see all the limit orders waiting to sell at higher prices ($100.06, $100.07, etc.).
- **The Bid Ladder:** Below the current price, you see all the limit orders waiting to buy at lower prices ($99.99, $99.98, etc.).

Crucially, this view reveals the *size* (liquidity) available at each level. Returning to our analogy: if Level 1 is the keyhole, Level 2 is opening the door wide. You might see that while the Best Bid is $100.00 for a small number of shares, there is a massive "wall" of buy orders waiting at $99.98.

This visibility changes a trader's perception of supply and demand. If you only see the BBO, the market might look balanced. But if the Depth-of-Book shows 50,000 shares wanted at $99.98 and only 500 shares for sale at $100.06, a professional knows that the price has strong support–it is harder for the price to fall than to rise. This "mountain" of resting orders acts as a buffer, information that is completely invisible to the retail trader staring at the simple Level 1 number.

By understanding the distinction between these feeds, we realize that market data is not just a record of what is happening; it is a map of what could happen next. The matching engine holds the truth of the entire book, but it only reveals the full picture to those who pay for the privilege of seeing it.

4.2 The Speed of Information: Latency and Staleness

In the previous section, we established that market data is not a monolithic entity but a tiered product, distinguishing between the limited view of Top-of-Book and the granular detail of Depth-of-Book. However, knowing *what* data you are seeing is only half the battle. The other, perhaps more critical dimension, is *when* you are seeing it.

To the human eye, a price blinking on a trading screen appears instantaneous. When the market moves, the numbers change. It feels like a live video stream of reality. But in the world of high-speed electronic trading, there is no such thing as "live." There is only history. By the time a photon emitted from your monitor hits your retina carrying the image of a price, that price is effectively an archaeological artifact. It describes a state of the world that existed in the past—a past that may be measured in milliseconds, but in modern markets, milliseconds are epochs.

This section explores the physics of finance. We will define latency not merely as "slowness" or a technical nuisance, but as the physical distance between truth and perception. We will trace the lifecycle of a price update to understand why the market you see on your screen often differs from the reality inside the matching engine, creating a phenomenon known as **staleness** or **phantom liquidity**.

Defining Latency: Distance as Time

In everyday computing, we think of latency as lag—the annoying pause when a website loads or a video buffers. In financial microstructure, latency is defined as the time elapsed between an event occurring in the matching engine (the "truth") and that information reaching an external observer (the "perception").

It is helpful to visualize the financial market not as a cloud, but as a specific physical location. The matching engine is a server sitting in a data center—say, in Secaucus, New Jersey, or Slough, outside of London. The "truth" of the market (the current bids, offers, and last trade price) exists strictly within the random-access memory (RAM) of that specific server.

If you are a trader sitting in an office in Chicago, you are bound by the laws of physics. Information cannot travel faster than the speed of light. In optical fiber, light travels at approximately two-thirds the speed of light in a vacuum. Therefore, even with a perfect, direct cable, it takes time for the "truth" to travel from New Jersey to Chicago.

However, distance is only one component. We must also account for processing time. The journey of a price update involves several distinct steps, each adding to the total latency:

- **Processing Latency (The Engine):** When a trade occurs, the matching engine must update its internal order book. It then has to "serialize" this update—converting the internal memory state into a standardized message format (like a binary protocol) suitable for transmission.
- **Transmission Latency (The Wire):** The message is sent out via a network interface card. It travels through switches and routers within the exchange's data center before hitting the wide-area network (WAN).
- **Propagation Delay (The Physics):** The signal travels through miles of fiber optic cable.
- **Deserialization and Display (The Client):** Your computer receives the packet. It must unpack (deserialize) the data, update

your trading software's internal model, and finally, your graphics card must redraw the pixels on your screen.

While the delay caused by step 4 might be 15 milliseconds—imperceptible to a human—an algorithmic trader located in the same building as the exchange might receive that data in 15 *microseconds*. This discrepancy creates a tiered reality where different participants perceive the "current" price at different times.

The Stale Zone and Phantom Liquidity

The most significant consequence of latency is the creation of "stale" quotes. A quote is considered stale when it is displayed on your screen, but the order it represents no longer exists in the matching engine.

Imagine you are looking at a Level 2 feed. You see 500 shares of Microsoft (MSFT) offered at $300.00. You decide this is a good price and click "Buy." A moment later, your platform plays a rejection sound or displays an error: "Order Rejected" or "Re-quoted at $300.01."

You might feel cheated. The screen clearly showed the shares were available. This experience is often referred to as chasing **phantom liquidity**.

Here is what actually happened. At Time T_0, the shares were indeed there. However, a high-frequency trading (HFT) algorithm—or simply a trader with a faster connection—saw that price and sent a buy order that arrived at the engine at $T_0 + 1\text{ms}$. The engine matched the order, consuming the 500 shares. The engine then sent out a message saying "The 500 shares at $300.00 are gone."

While that "delete" message was traveling through the internet to your computer, you were still looking at the "add" message from earlier. You were looking at a star that had already burned out. This interval, between the moment the engine state changes and the moment you receive the update, is the **Stale Zone**.

Any decision you make based on data in the Stale Zone is a decision made on false premises. You are attempting to trade against a market that no longer exists.

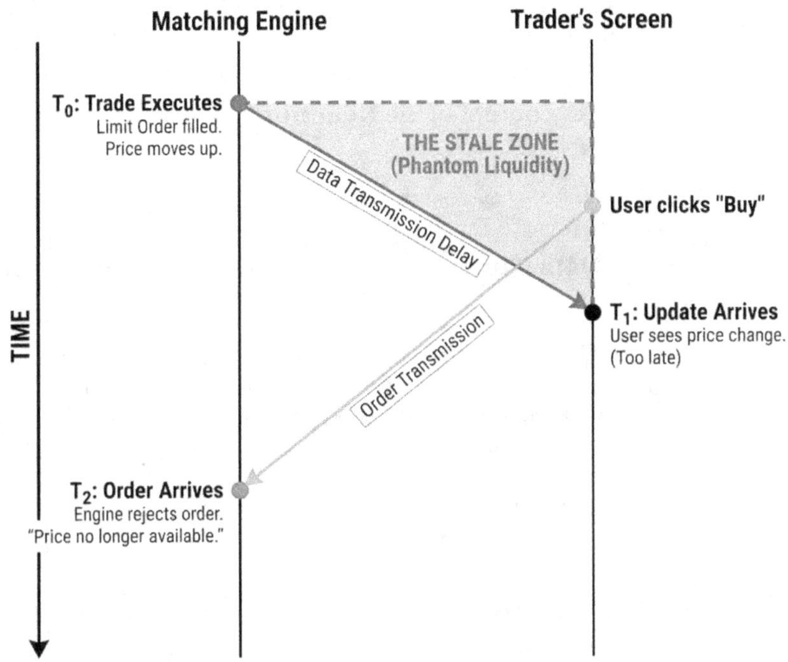

The diagram below illustrates this "Event Horizon." At T_0, the engine matches a trade, and the price changes. However, the trader at the screen is unaware of this change until T_1. The triangular region between T_0 and T_1 represents the danger zone. During this period, the trader's screen shows the *old* price. If the trader clicks "Buy" during this window (indicated by the orange dot), they are reacting to a mirage. Their order travels back to the engine, arriving at T_2, only to be rejected because the liquidity they sought was consumed back at T_0.

The Round Trip: The Cost of Reaction

It is important to understand that speed in trading is measured as a round-trip ticket. It is not enough to simply *see* the price; you must be able to send an order back to the exchange before anyone else does.

This brings us to the concept of the **Reaction Loop**.

$$T_{total} = T_{inbound} + T_{decision} + T_{outbound}$$

- **Inbound Data Time:** The time for the market data to reach you.
- **Decision Time:** The time it takes your brain (or your computer code) to process that data and decide to act. For a human, simple reaction time to visual stimuli is roughly 200 to 250 milliseconds. For a computer, it can be measured in nanoseconds.
- **Outbound Order Time:** The time for your "Buy" order to travel back to the exchange.

If you are a discretionary trader (a human clicking buttons), your "Decision Time" is the bottleneck. Even if you had a direct fiber optic line to the exchange that delivered data instantly, your brain's processing speed makes you roughly 200,000 times slower than a high-frequency algorithm.

This is why "scalping" (trying to capture very small price movements) based on the visual tape is incredibly difficult for retail traders. By the time your brain registers that a large buy order has hit the tape, automated systems have already processed that information, sent their own orders, and moved the price. You are effectively watching a replay of a game that ended seconds ago.

Implications for the Trader

Does this mean the market is "rigged" or that you cannot trade successfully? No. It simply means you must understand the nature of the data you are viewing.

For long-term investors or swing traders, latency is negligible. Whether you buy Apple stock at $150.00 or $150.05 matters little if your target is $200.00. The "stale" nature of the price is a rounding error in your thesis.

However, for active traders relying on short-term momentum or order flow, acknowledging latency is vital. It explains why market orders sometimes fill at worse prices than expected (slippage) and why limit orders placed at the current Best Bid often sit unfilled while the market trades around them. You are viewing a projection of the past, and to interact with the market successfully, you must anticipate where the price is going to be when your order arrives, not just where it appears to be right now.

4.3 Trade Reporting and the Tape

If the market data feeds discussed in the previous section represent the *intent* to trade–buyers and sellers shouting their prices across the room–then the "Tape" represents the *result*. It is the history book of the market. While quotes tell you what might happen next, the Tape tells you exactly what just happened.

For most of the 20th century, this was literal: a ticker tape machine printed abbreviated company names and prices on a strip of paper. Today, the "Tape" is a digital stream of execution reports. However, for the casual observer, there is often a confusing discrepancy between the price they see on the screen (the quote) and the price at which trades actually occur. To understand this, we must look at how the matching engine decides which trades are *important* enough to change the official market price.

The Receipt vs. The Billboard

When a matching engine successfully pairs a buyer and a seller, two things happen almost simultaneously. First, the engine sends a private confirmation to the two parties involved; this is your personal receipt. Second, the engine broadcasts a public report to the Consolidated Tape; this is the public announcement.

The Consolidated Tape (often referred to as the SIP, or Securities Information Processor) aggregates these trade reports from all exchanges—NYSE, NASDAQ, BATS, and others—into a single stream. This is where the "Last Traded Price" on your brokerage app comes from.

However, not every trade is treated equally when it comes to updating the *quoted* price of a stock. This leads to one of the most common questions from new traders: *"Why did a trade happen at a price better than the one I see on my screen?"* The answer often lies in the distinction between Round Lots and Odd Lots.

Round Lots: The Standard Unit

Historically, stocks were physically difficult to transfer. To maintain efficiency, exchanges established a standard unit of trading, known as a **Round Lot**. For the vast majority of stocks, a Round Lot is 100 shares.

The matching engine views Round Lots as the "official" liquidity of the market. When you see the "National Best Bid and Offer" (NBBO)—the standard benchmark price for a stock—it is calculated almost exclusively using Round Lots.

If a bank places a limit order to buy 100 shares at $50.00, that order is broadcast to the world. It updates the public quote. It tells the market, "There is significant demand here."

Odd Lots: The Invisible Trades

An **Odd Lot** is any order size smaller than the standard Round Lot—usually between 1 and 99 shares. This is the domain of the average retail investor. If you buy 15 shares of Apple or 50 shares of Microsoft, you are trading an Odd Lot.

Here is the crucial distinction: Historically, and in many current data feed configurations, **Odd Lot orders do not update the official Best Bid or Offer.**

Imagine the current market for a stock looks like this:

- **Best Bid:** $10.00 (Size: 100 shares)

- **Best Ask:** $10.05 (Size: 100 shares)

Now, suppose you enter a Limit Order to buy 50 shares at $10.02. In the matching engine, your order sits at $10.02, logically ahead of the $10.00 bid. You are willing to pay more. However, because your order is an Odd Lot (under 100 shares), the public quote feed often ignores it. The official "Best Bid" remains displayed as $10.00.

To the outside world, your order is invisible on the top-level price board. It exists in the engine, and if a seller sends a market order, you will get filled at $10.02. When that trade executes, the Tape will report a trade at $10.02.

The Confusion of "Printing" the Trade

This mechanism creates a scenario that looks like a glitch to the uninitiated. A trader watching their screen sees the price quoted at $10.00. Suddenly, the "Last Trade" ticker flashes $10.02, but the Buy Price stays stuck at $10.00.

The trader thinks, *"The price went up to $10.02, why can't I sell there?"* The reality is that the $10.02 price was a small, Odd Lot transaction. It "printed" to the Tape (the history), but it was insufficient to move the Quote (the billboard).

This distinction is vital for understanding market visibility. While the matching engine treats all orders mathematically—matching a sell order against the highest buy price regardless of size—the reporting logic filters what the broad market sees to prevent noise. As retail trading grows and high-priced stocks make 100-share blocks expensive, regulators and exchanges are slowly evolving these definitions, but for now, the gap between the "Official Price" (Round Lots) and the "Actual Trading Activity" (including Odd Lots) remains a distinct feature of market structure.

4.4 Microstructure Dynamics: Queues and Adverse Selection

Up to this point, we have looked at the market as observers. We have examined the depth of data feeds and measured the invisible delays of latency. But trading is not a spectator sport. Eventually, you must participate. You must send an order into the engine and wait for a result.

This transition—from watching the screen to entering the market—introduces a new set of physical realities. When you place a limit order (an order to buy or sell at a specific price), you do not simply magically interact with a seller. You enter a physical space inside the matching engine memory. You join a **queue**.

Understanding the dynamics of this queue, and who is standing in line with you, is the key to understanding one of the most painful lessons in trading: why your orders often fail to fill when you want them to, and why they fill instantly when you wish they hadn't.

Life in the Queue

Imagine a bakery that sells only one specific type of bread at a fixed price. Customers who want to buy the bread line up at the counter. The baker (the market) serves them in the order they arrived: First-In, First-Out (FIFO).

In the stock market, every price level is a separate counter with its own line. If Apple stock is trading at $150.00, and you place a limit order to buy at $149.95, you are joining the queue at the $149.95 price node. If there are already 5,000 shares ordered at that price before you arrived, those 5,000 shares must be satisfied before you get a single share.

This position in line is your **queue priority**.

On a professional trader's screen (Level 2 data), you might see that there are 10,000 shares bidding at $149.95. What the screen doesn't explicitly tell you is where *you* are in that pile. You might be at the front, meaning the next 100 shares sold will be yours. Or you might be at the very back, meaning you are effectively an insurance policy for everyone ahead of you—you will only get filled if the selling pressure is strong enough to chew through everyone else first.

The Winner's Curse

This brings us to the dark side of limit orders. In a perfect world, you want to buy low and sell high. You place a buy order at a price slightly below the current market, hoping the price dips just enough to fill you, and then bounces back up.

However, the market is an adversarial environment. There are informed traders—institutions, algorithms, and market makers—who spend millions of dollars on faster data and better prediction models. If they decide to sell to you, it is usually because they believe the price is about to go lower.

This phenomenon is known as **Adverse Selection**.

Think of it this way: You are offering to buy insurance on a house (the stock) for a fixed premium (your limit price). If the skies are clear, nobody wants to sell you that insurance; they want to keep the house. But if a hurricane is visible on the horizon—information that the *smart money* sees before you do—suddenly everyone wants to sell you the house.

The Toxic Fill

The moment of execution is where the difference between retail perception and microstructure reality becomes stark.

A **toxic fill** occurs when your limit order is executed immediately before the price moves against you. You are sitting in the queue at $10.00. For an hour, the price hovers at $10.01, and you get no shares. Suddenly, a massive sell order comes in. It smashes through the buy orders at $10.01 and continues down to $10.00.

The "smart money" aggressor eats through the queue at $10.00. They eat the first order, the second order, and then they hit you. You are filled. You own the stock at $10.00.

One millisecond later, the Best Bid drops to $9.99.

You got exactly what you asked for—a fill at your price—but you got it at the worst possible time. You were the "liquidity of last resort" for someone who was exiting the building before it collapsed. The queue didn't just serve you; it trapped you. The orders ahead of you provided a buffer, but once they were gone, you were left standing on the edge of a cliff just as the ground gave way.

This dynamic explains a common frustration for new traders: "Why does the market bounce when I don't get filled, and crash when I do?" The answer is that the fill itself is often a signal that the opposing side has overwhelming conviction.

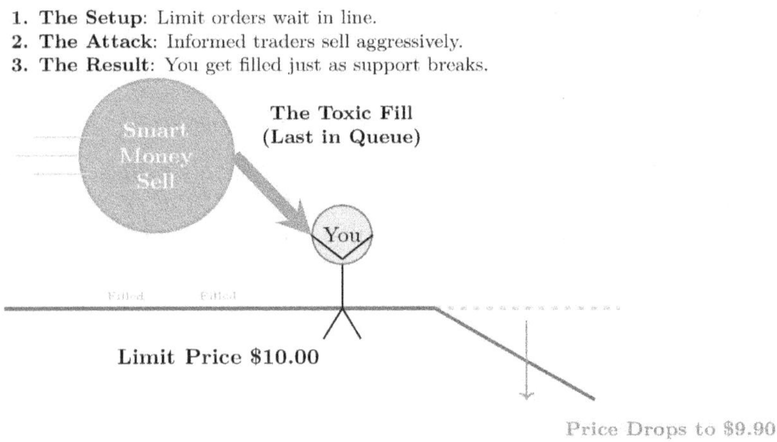

This diagram illustrates the mechanism of regret. The "Smart Money" wrecking ball—representing a large, informed market order—smashes through the queue. The orders at the front absorb the initial impact, but if the selling pressure is strong enough, it reaches you. By the time your order is executed, the protective wall of liquidity that stood in front of you is gone. You are now the new best bid, but only for a fraction of a second before the floor gives way and the price crashes.

In the ecosystem of the matching engine, visibility is survival. Understanding that a limit order is not just a price request, but a position in a vulnerable line, is the first step toward avoiding the trap of adverse selection.

Chapter 5

The Journey to the Exchange: Routing and Economics

When you click 'buy', your order doesn't just teleport to a stock exchange; it enters a high-speed logistical web. Before reaching a matching engine, your trade must navigate a fragmented landscape of over a dozen exchanges and countless dark pools. This chapter lifts the hood on the Smart Order Router (SOR)-the GPS of the trading world-and reveals the complex economic incentives, from rebates to payments for order flow, that determine the path your money takes.

5.1 The Broker's Challenge: Best Execution

When you tap "Buy" on your phone screen to purchase 100 shares of a company, the interface is designed to feel as simple as buying a book online. You see a price, you confirm the transaction, and moments later, you own the stock. But unlike a digital bookstore where the inventory sits in a known warehouse at a fixed price, the stock market is a dynamic, shifting ecosystem of millions of competing desires.

Behind that "Buy" button lies a complex web of decision-making. You, the investor, are not actually walking into the exchange to buy the stock yourself. Instead, you are hiring an agent-your broker-to go into the market on your behalf. This relationship is defined by a critical legal and ethical obligation known as **Best Execution**.

To understand Best Execution, imagine you send a friend to the grocery store to buy apples. You give them twenty dollars and a simple instruction: "Get me the best deal on ten apples." If your friend returns ten minutes later with ten bruised apples that cost two dollars each, purchased from the expensive convenience store across the street because they didn't want to walk further, you would be rightfully upset. You know that a large supermarket three blocks away sells fresh, crisp apples for fifty cents. Your friend failed their duty; they prioritized their own convenience (a short walk) over your outcome (price and quality).

In financial markets, the broker is that friend. However, the definition of a "good deal" in trading is far more nuanced than just the price tag on an apple. When a broker receives your order, they face a multidimensional optimization problem. They must balance three competing forces: **Price**, **Speed**, and **Certainty**.

The Three Pillars of Execution Quality

The most obvious metric for a good trade is **Price**. If the market is trading a stock around $100.00, and your broker buys it for you at $100.01, that seems acceptable. If they buy it at $100.50, they have failed you. This is "price improvement"-getting a price equal to or better than the best displayed price in the market.

However, price cannot be viewed in isolation. This brings us to the second pillar: **Speed**. Financial markets move in microseconds. A price of $100.00 might be available right now, but in half a second, good news about the company could hit the wires, sending the price up to $100.20. If your broker delays execution to hunt for a strictly "better" price (say, trying to buy at $99.99), they might miss the $100.00 opportunity entirely and end up buying at $100.20 when the market runs away. In this scenario, a faster execution at a slightly higher initial price would have been the better outcome. This cost of waiting is often called "slippage."

The third pillar is **Certainty**, or the likelihood of execution. Imagine you want to buy 1,000 shares. There might be an offer to sell 100 shares at $100.00 and an offer to sell 5,000 shares at $100.05. If the broker rigidly insists on the lowest price, they fill only 100 shares. If the stock price then rises, you are left holding a mostly empty bag, having missed the opportunity to acquire the full position. A strategy prioritizing certainty might sweep the market, paying a slightly higher average price (perhaps $100.04) to ensure you possess the full 1,000 shares immediately.

The Broker's Dilemma

Balancing these three pillars is the heart of the broker's challenge. There is no single "correct" answer that applies to every trade. A retail investor buying $500 worth of stock usually prioritizes price improvement above all else. A large institutional pension fund buying $50 million worth of stock prioritizes discretion and certainty; they want to get the trade done without alerting other traders, which would cause the price to spike before they finish buying.

Complicating this further is the broker's own business model. Connecting to exchanges costs money. Sending orders to certain venues incurs fees, while others might offer rebates (a topic we will explore later in the chapter). This creates a potential conflict of interest. A broker might be tempted to route your order to the venue that pays them the highest rebate, rather than the venue that offers you the best price or fastest fill.

Regulators are acutely aware of this tension. In the United States, Regulation NMS (National Market System) and FINRA rules legally mandate that brokers must use "reasonable diligence" to ascertain the best market for the subject security so that the resultant price to the customer is as favorable as possible. Brokers must regularly review their routing practices and prove that they are not systematically disadvantaging clients to save on costs.

The Technology of Choice

To satisfy this obligation, brokers cannot rely on human traders making phone calls. The speed of modern markets renders manual routing impossible. Instead, brokers employ sophisticated algorithms known as **Smart Order Routers (SORs)**.

The SOR is the "brain" of the execution process. It is a software engine that maintains a real-time map of the entire market. It knows which exchanges are currently offering stock, at what price, and in what quantity. When you click "Buy," the SOR instantly evaluates the state of the market against the criteria of Best Execution. It decides within microseconds whether to send your order to the New York Stock Exchange, Nasdaq, a specialized electronic venue, or a wholesaler.

This automated decision-making is the bridge between your intention to trade and the actual exchange of assets. However, for an SOR to work, it needs a destination. It cannot simply send an order to "the stock market" because, as we will see in the next section, "the market" is not a single building or computer. It is a fragmented network of dozens of different venues, all shouting prices at the same time. The first step in routing is understanding this fractured landscape and how a single, unified price is constructed from the noise.

5.2 Fragmentation and the Consolidated Price

When you check a stock price on a smartphone or watch a ticker scroll across the bottom of a television screen, you are seeing a single, clean number. If shares of General Electric are displayed at $100.00, it feels as though that is the only price in existence. This simplicity, however, is an illusion constructed by the market infrastructure.

In reality, there is no single building or computer where "the market" lives. The U.S. stock market is heavily fragmented. It is a scattered network of over a dozen public exchanges (like the New York Stock Exchange, Nasdaq, IEX, and CBOE) and dozens of private trading venues. At any given millisecond, a share of General Electric might be on sale for $100.00 at a data center in Mahwah, New Jersey (NYSE), while simultaneously on sale for $100.01 at a data center in Carteret, New Jersey (Nasdaq).

This fragmentation creates a significant problem for the broker we discussed in the previous section. If the broker needs to buy shares for a client, they cannot simply "go to the market." They must decide *which* market to visit. More importantly, how does the broker-and the general public-know which price is the "real" price?

To solve this, the financial industry relies on a centralized data feed known as the **Securities Information Processor**, or simply the **SIP**.

You can think of the SIP as the "great aggregator." Every public exchange is legally required to send its best buy and sell orders to the SIP in real-time. The SIP acts like a high-speed funnel: it intakes millions of price updates from all the different venues, compares them instantly, and outputs a single "official" price stream.

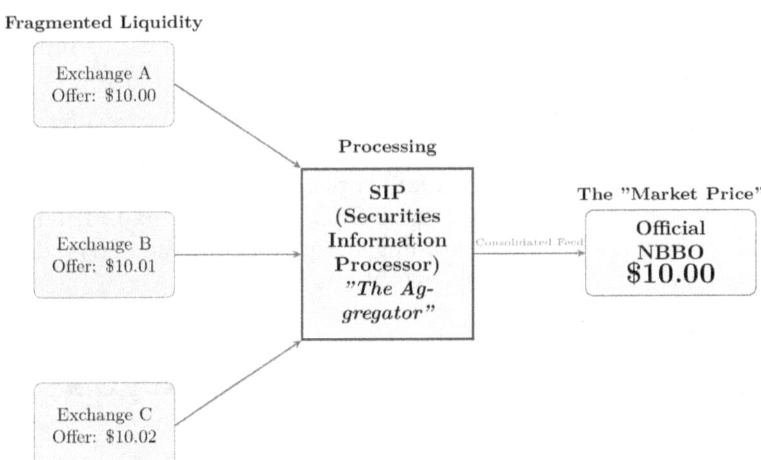

The output of this process is what traders call the **NBBO**: the **National Best Bid and Offer**.

The NBBO is the golden standard of stock pricing. It is a dynamic construct composed of two numbers:

- **National Best Bid**: The highest price anyone across all exchanges is currently willing to pay to *buy* the stock.
- **National Best Offer**: The lowest price anyone across all exchanges is currently willing to accept to *sell* the stock.

Using the example in the diagram above, Exchange A is offering to sell the stock at $10.00, while Exchanges B and C are asking for $10.01 and $10.02. The SIP reads these inputs and determines that $10.00 is the lowest available price. Consequently, $10.00 becomes the National Best Offer.

This system is enforced by a federal regulation known as **Reg NMS** (Regulation National Market System). One of the core tenets of Reg NMS is the "Trade-Through Rule." This rule prohibits a trading venue from executing an order at a price inferior to the NBBO.

In simple terms, if you send a buy order to Exchange C (where the price is $10.02), Exchange C is generally not allowed to fill your order at $10.02 if Exchange A is showing a price of $10.00. Instead, the system must ensure you get the $10.00 price, or the order must be routed to the venue holding that price.

This creates a virtual unification of the market. Even though the servers are miles apart and run by competing corporations, the NBBO forces them to act as a single liquidity pool. For the smart order router-the software the broker uses-the NBBO acts as the map. It tells the router where the best price is hiding, turning the fragmented landscape into a navigable path for best execution.

5.3 Smart Order Routing Strategies

In the previous section, we established that the "market" is not a single location but a fragmented network of exchanges and data centers. We also explained how the SIP produces the National Best Bid and Offer (NBBO)–the "official" price tag that dictates the best available price across all venues.

However, knowing the price is only half the battle. The second half is actually securing the stock. This is where the **Smart Order Router**

(SOR) comes into play.

If the NBBO is the destination on a map, the SOR is the GPS navigation system. Just as a GPS calculates the optimal path based on traffic, road closures, and speed limits, the SOR analyzes the fragmented market landscape to decide exactly where to send your order to get the best result. It is an algorithmic decision-making engine that sits between the broker and the exchanges, operating at microsecond speeds.

The Challenge of Fragmentation

Imagine you want to buy 1,000 shares of a company. The NBBO displays a price of $50.00. However, because liquidity is fragmented, those 1,000 shares are likely not sitting on a single exchange.

- Exchange A has 400 shares at $50.00.
- Exchange B has 300 shares at $50.00.
- Exchange C has 300 shares at $50.00.

A naive approach would be to send an order for 1,000 shares to Exchange A. However, Exchange A only has 400 shares. You would buy those 400, but the remaining 600 shares of your order would likely be posted on Exchange A's book, signaling to the world that there is a buyer in town. High-frequency traders might see this signal and immediately buy up the cheap shares on Exchanges B and C, intending to sell them back to you at $50.01. This is known as "market impact" or "information leakage."

To avoid this, the SOR breaks the "parent" order (1,000 shares) into smaller "child" orders.

The Sweep Strategy

When a trader values speed and certainty of execution above all else, the router employs a **Sweep** strategy. This is an aggressive tactic designed to capture all available liquidity at a specific price point simultaneously across multiple venues.

In our example, the SOR analyzes the depth of the market and calculates exactly how many shares are available at $50.00 on every exchange. It then fires three simultaneous child orders: 400 to Exchange A, 300 to Exchange B, and 300 to Exchange C.

The goal is to hit all three venues at the exact same millisecond. If the router is too slow–if the order hits Exchange A before the others–computers monitoring Exchange A's data feed will react before the orders reach B and C. This requires sophisticated technology that accounts for the physical distance of fiber-optic cables between data centers, delaying the closer orders slightly so that they all arrive at the finish line in unison.

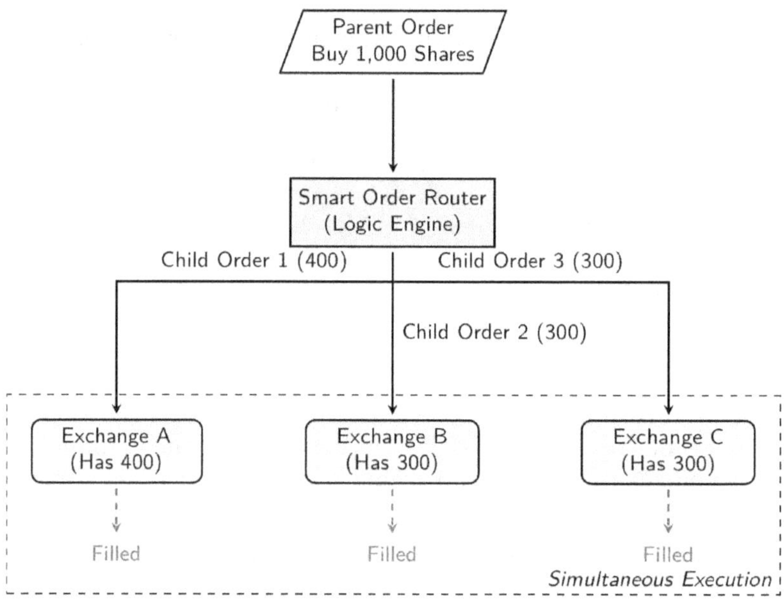

Serial Routing and Slicing

Not all strategies are aggressive. Sometimes, a router wants to minimize costs or hide intention rather than maximize speed.

In a **Serial** or "Waterfall" strategy, the router pings venues one by one.

It might check a "dark pool" (a private exchange where orders are hidden) first to see if it can get a better price. If that fails, it moves to the public exchange with the lowest fees. If that fails, it finally goes to the exchange with the most liquidity. This process is slower and risks missing the price if the market moves quickly, but it can significantly reduce transaction costs.

For very large orders–say, buying 100,000 shares–routers use **Slicing** algorithms (often called "Icebergs"). Instead of showing the full size, the router releases a small "tip" of the order (e.g., 100 shares) to the market. Once those are filled, it reloads with another 100 shares. This prevents the market from panicking and driving the price up in response to massive demand.

The choice between sweeping, spraying, or slicing depends heavily on the economics of the trade. Why would a router choose one exchange over another if the price is identical? The answer lies in the complex system of maker-taker fees, which we will explore in the next section.

5.4 The Economics of Flow: Fees and Rebates

In the previous section, we explored how Smart Order Routers (SORs) slice and sweep orders to navigate the fragmented landscape of modern markets. We visualized the router as a sophisticated GPS, seeking the fastest or most probable path to execution. However, in financial markets, the "best" path isn't determined solely by the speed of the road or the likelihood of arrival. There is a toll booth on every highway, and curiously, some of these toll booths actually pay you to drive through them.

To understand why a router chooses one exchange over another, we must look beyond the technology and examine the business model of the exchanges themselves. This brings us to one of the most significant, yet frequently misunderstood, forces in market structure: the **Maker-Taker pricing model**.

Liquidity: The Service of Waiting

To grasp Maker-Taker pricing, we must first revisit the concept of liquidity. In our earlier chapters, we defined liquidity as the ability to buy or sell an asset easily. But in the context of exchange economics, liquidity is a service provided by one group of traders and consumed by another.

Imagine a specialized grocery store that has empty shelves. The store owner (the exchange) does not buy the inventory. Instead, they rely on independent merchants to place apples, bread, and milk on the shelves.

- **The Maker:** A merchant who places a product on the shelf and waits for a buyer is "making" inventory. In trading, this is the trader who posts a **Limit Order** that rests on the order book. They are adding liquidity to the market.
- **The Taker:** A customer who walks in, sees the product, and immediately buys it is "taking" inventory. In trading, this is the trader who sends a **Market Order** (or a marketable limit order) that matches immediately with an existing order. They are removing liquidity from the market.

The distinction is crucial because the Maker takes on risk. By posting a limit order to buy 100 shares of Microsoft at $300.00, the Maker is revealing their hand to the world and waiting. The market might move against them while they sit there. The Taker, conversely, gets immediate gratification. They transfer their risk instantly to the Maker.

The Fee and Rebate Mechanism

Because the Maker provides a valuable service—stocking the shelves so trade can happen—exchanges created a pricing structure to incentivize them. They reasoned that if they paid traders to post orders, their exchange would have the deepest order book, attracting more investors.

This is the Maker-Taker model. It typically works like this:

- 1. **The Taker Fee:** The aggressive trader who crosses the spread to buy stock pays a fee to the exchange. For example, the exchange might charge the Taker $0.0030 per share.

- 2. **The Maker Rebate:** The passive trader whose order was sitting on the book receives a payment from the exchange. The exchange might pay the Maker $0.0020 per share.
- 3. **The Exchange's Profit:** The exchange collects 30 "mils" (market slang for thousandths of a dollar) from the Taker, pays 20 mils to the Maker, and keeps the 10-mil difference as their revenue.

It is a stunning realization for many new to the industry: sophisticated trading firms are often paid to trade. If a high-frequency trading firm or a market maker posts millions of shares a day, those tiny fractions of a penny accumulate into substantial revenue.

The Conflict of Interest in Routing

This economic structure fundamentally alters the logic of the Smart Order Router. Recall the broker's challenge of "Best Execution." The broker is legally obligated to find the best outcome for the client. However, the broker is also a business that needs to manage its own costs.

Consider a scenario where a client sends a market order to buy 1,000 shares. The router sees the exact same price, $50.00, available at two different exchanges:

- **Exchange A** charges a Taker fee of $0.0030 per share.
- **Exchange B** charges a Taker fee of $0.0028 per share.

If the broker routes the order to Exchange A, it costs the broker $3.00. If they route to Exchange B, it costs $2.80. While twenty cents seems trivial on a single trade, multiplied across millions of shares daily, it dictates profitability. Consequently, routers are programmed to be fee-sensitive.

The situation becomes even more complex when handling limit orders for clients. If a client wants to buy 1,000 shares at $50.00 and is willing to wait (making them a Maker), the broker now has a choice of where to post that order.

- **Exchange A** offers a Maker rebate of $0.0020 per share.

- **Exchange B** offers a Maker rebate of $0.0029 per share.

The broker is heavily incentivized to route the client's order to Exchange B to capture the higher rebate. This practice is standard and legal, provided that Exchange B is a valid venue. However, critics argue that this creates a conflict: perhaps Exchange A has a higher fill rate (likelihood of execution), but the router chose Exchange B solely for the economic kickback.

Inverted Venues

To further complicate the landscape, some exchanges operate an **Inverted** or "Taker-Maker" model. In this setup, the economics are reversed: the exchange charges the Maker for the privilege of posting an order and pays a rebate to the Taker who removes it.

Why would anyone pay to post an order when other exchanges pay you to do it? The answer is queue priority. Because most Makers flock to the high-rebate exchanges, the line to buy stock at the best price can be extremely long—sometimes thousands of orders deep. On an inverted exchange that charges a fee to post, the line is much shorter. A trader who urgently needs to buy stock at a specific limit price might pay the fee on an inverted venue just to be at the front of the line, ensuring they get filled before the price moves away.

The Aggregate Impact

The Maker-Taker model explains why there is so much "noise" in market data. Much of the quoting activity (changing bids and offers) is the result of algorithms jockeying for queue position to capture rebates.

For the everyday investor, these fees are invisible. When you buy a share on a retail app, you do not see a line item for "Exchange Access Fee" or a credit for "Liquidity Rebate." Your broker absorbs these costs and collects these revenues. However, understanding this flow of funds is essential to understanding why your order went to the NASDAQ instead of the NYSE, or to a smaller exchange like CBOE EDGX. The invisible hand of the market is often guided by the invisible price tag of the venue.

5.5 Off-Exchange Execution and Wholesalers

So far, we have explored the market as if it were a single, albeit fragmented, public utility. We have discussed how Smart Order Routers (SORs) scour public exchanges like the NYSE or Nasdaq to find the best price, navigating a landscape of Maker-Taker fees and rebates. However, if you open a brokerage app on your phone and buy ten shares of a popular tech stock, it is highly unlikely that your order will ever interact with those public exchanges.

Instead, your order will likely be handled through a completely different mechanism known as **internalization**. This segment of the market operates away from the "lit" public exchanges, often referred to as "off-exchange" or "dark" trading, though in the context of retail investing, it is more accurately described as the wholesale market.

To understand why this happens, we must look at the market through the eyes of a market maker.

The Retail vs. Institutional Distinction

In the previous section on Smart Order Routing, we implicitly focused on institutional investors—pension funds, mutual funds, and hedge funds moving large blocks of shares. When a large institution buys stock, they tend to move the market. If a hedge fund wants to buy 100,000 shares, that demand signals that the price is likely to rise. For a market maker, selling to a large institution is risky; they might sell stock at $50.00 only to see the price immediately jump to $50.10, forcing them to buy it back at a loss.

Retail orders—the kind placed by individual investors—are different. They are typically small (often just a handful of shares) and, statistically speaking, they are "uninformed." This does not mean retail investors are not smart; it means their buying activity usually isn't a signal that the stock price is about to shift fundamentally in the next millisecond.

Because retail flow is safer and less volatile to trade against, market making firms (wholesalers) compete aggressively to execute these orders. They want your order so badly that they are willing to pay your broker for the privilege of executing it.

Payment for Order Flow (PFOF)

This dynamic gave rise to a practice called Payment for Order Flow (PFOF). Instead of sending your order to a public exchange (where they might have to pay a "take" fee), your broker routes your order directly to a wholesaler—a firm like Citadel Securities or Virtu Financial.

The wholesaler acts as a counterparty. If you are buying, the wholesaler sells to you from their own inventory. If you are selling, they buy from you. In exchange for this steady stream of "safe" orders, the wholesaler pays a small fee back to the brokerage firm. This revenue stream is a primary reason why many retail brokerages are able to offer zero-commission trading.

Price Improvement: The Benefit to the Trader

If the broker is getting paid to route your order to a specific firm, you might naturally worry that you are getting a bad deal. Is this a conflict of interest?

To mitigate this, regulations require that wholesalers provide **Best Execution**. In the context of internalization, this usually manifests as **Price Improvement**. The wholesaler cannot fill your order at a price worse than the National Best Bid and Offer (NBBO) currently displayed on the public exchanges. In fact, to justify intercepting the order, they often improve upon it.

Imagine the NBBO for a stock is:

- **Bid:** $10.00 (The highest price someone is willing to pay)
- **Offer:** $10.01 (The lowest price someone is willing to sell)

If you place a market order to buy, a public exchange would execute you at the Offer price of $10.01. However, the wholesaler might step in and sell the stock to you at **$10.009**.

While a savings of a fraction of a cent per share sounds negligible, it adds up over millions of shares. For the wholesaler, selling at $10.009 is still profitable if they can buy the stock elsewhere at $10.00 or if they are simply capturing the spread. For you, the price is strictly better than what was available on the public market.

The Two Paths of Execution

We can now visualize the stock market as a system with two distinct highways.

The first is the **Institutional Path**. This is the domain of sophisticated algorithms, Smart Order Routers, and public exchanges. Here, routers slice large orders into pieces, hunting for liquidity across Nasdaq, NYSE, and dark pools, paying execution fees, and battling for queue position.

The second is the **Retail Path**. This is a concierge service. The order bypasses the public highway entirely. It is routed directly to a wholesaler who executes it instantly, often at a price slightly better than the public benchmark, funded by the economics of the spread and payment for order flow.

The following diagram illustrates these divergent journeys and highlights the trade-offs involved in each.

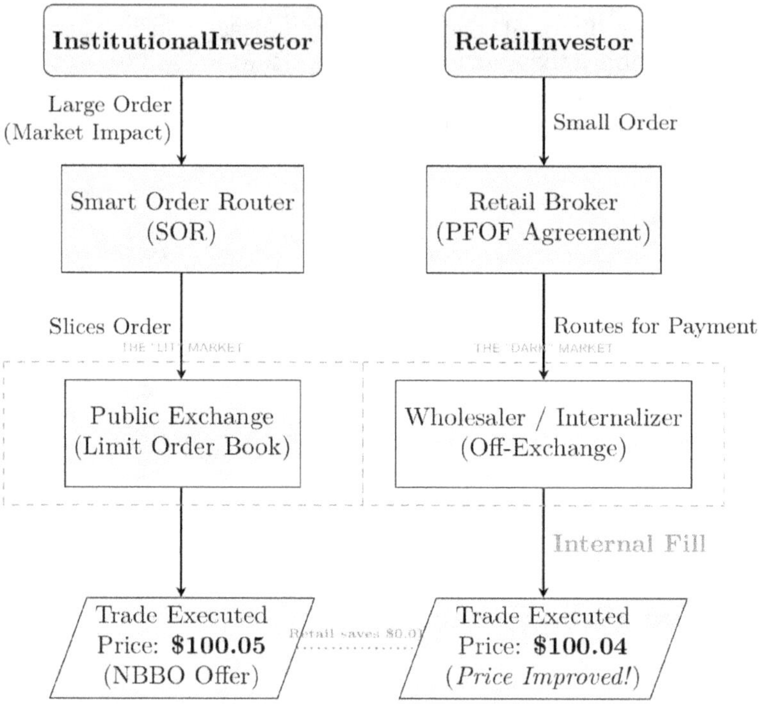

The journey of an order depends entirely on who sends it. While the backbone of the stock market consists of the matching engines, auctions, and consolidated feeds we discussed earlier in this chapter, a significant portion of daily volume never touches that infrastructure directly.

Wholesalers act as shock absorbers for retail flow, providing immediate liquidity and price improvement in exchange for the ability to capture the bid-ask spread on lower-risk orders. Meanwhile, institutional flow battles it out in the public arena, relying on sophisticated routing algorithms to minimize impact and costs. Understanding these two paths is essential to understanding the modern market structure: it is not just one destination, but a network of competing venues, each with its own economic incentives.

Chapter 6

Execution in Practice: Scenarios and Reality

We have dismantled the matching engine, inspected the order types, and timed the cables. Now, it is time to put the machine in motion. In this concluding chapter, we leave the theoretical 'clean room' and enter the messy, high-speed reality of the live market. We will follow orders as they navigate fragmented venues, fight for queue position, and settle in the closing auction, ultimately answering the trader's most pressing question: 'Why did my trade happen at that price?'

6.1 Scenario: Aggressive Execution in a Fast Market

When you press the "Buy" button on your trading screen, the action feels instantaneous. A confirmation window pops up, the shares appear in your account, and your cash balance drops. It is clean, simple, and deceptive. The seamlessness of the user interface hides a violent and fragmented struggle occurring in the milliseconds between your click and the confirmation.

To understand the reality of execution, we must leave the calm of the user interface and enter the machinery of a "Fast Market." In this scenario, we assume you are a trader looking to buy 1,000 shares of a popular stock, "XYZ Corp," currently trading at $100.00. You enter a **Market Order**, which is an instruction to buy immediately at whatever price the market offers. You are prioritizing speed over price.

The first challenge your order faces is fragmentation. There is no single "stock market" where all shares of XYZ Corp live. Instead, liquidity is scattered across multiple venues-perhaps 300 shares are waiting on the New York Stock Exchange (NYSE), 400 on Nasdaq, and another 300 on a secondary exchange like CBOE or a dark pool. The price of $100.00 you saw on your screen is an aggregation, a "best of" summary compiled from these disparate sources.

The Split: Smart Order Routing (SOR)

Your broker's system does not simply send your order to the NYSE and hope for the best. If it did, you would buy the 300 shares available there, but the remaining 700 shares of your order would be unfilled, or worse, forced to buy the next available shares on NYSE at a much higher price (e.g., $100.05).

Instead, your order passes through a **Smart Order Router (SOR)**. The SOR is an algorithm acting as a high-speed dispatcher. It looks at the consolidated market feed and creates a "routing map." It calculates that to fill your 1,000 shares efficiently, it must simultaneously target the liquidity pools at all three venues.

The SOR slices your single **Parent** order into three **Child** orders:

- **Child A:** Buy 300 shares at NYSE (Price $100.00).
- **Child B:** Buy 400 shares at Nasdaq (Price $100.01).
- **Child C:** Buy 300 shares at CBOE (Price $100.02).

Notice that the prices are different. This is the first mechanical reality of aggressive execution: **Walking the Book**. Because the cheapest shares ($100.00) were insufficient to fill your entire order, the SOR had to reach for more expensive shares to complete the trade.

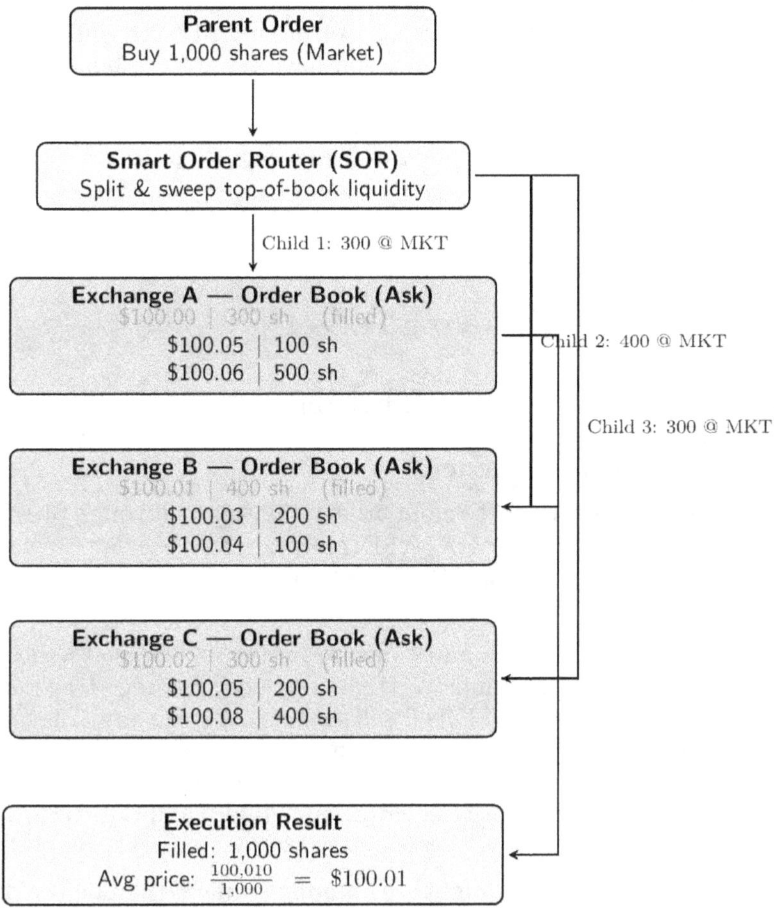

Slippage: The Hidden Cost

The phenomenon described above results in **Slippage**. While the "Best Bid/Offer" (BBO) on the screen showed $100.00, your realized price—the average price you actually paid—was $100.01.

This discrepancy occurs because the "Price" of a stock is not a single, solid number. It is a thin layer of liquidity at the top of a stack. When your order is larger than that top layer, you break through the surface and consume orders deeper in the stack (the Order Book), where prices are worse. In professional terms, you have "swept the book." For a retail trader buying 10 shares, this is rarely noticeable. For an institutional algorithm buying 10,000 shares, slippage is a primary cost of doing business, often exceeding the cost of commissions.

Latency and the Moving Target

The scenario above assumes a perfect world where the market stands still while you trade. In reality, the market is a moving target. This introduces the risk of **Latency**.

When the SOR fires its three child orders, they travel through fiber optic cables to the data centers of NYSE (Mahwah, NJ), Nasdaq (Carteret, NJ), and CBOE (Secaucus, NJ). These locations are miles apart. Light travels fast, but not instantly.

If Child A arrives at NYSE and consumes the 300 shares at $100.00, that trade is broadcast publicly. High-frequency trading (HFT) algorithms monitoring the NYSE feed will see this trade execute. They may instantly deduce that a large buyer is in the market sweeping liquidity. These algorithms can race ahead to Nasdaq and CBOE to cancel their sell orders or raise their prices before your Child B and Child C orders arrive.

This is often why a trader might see liquidity "vanish" right before they can grab it. If your Child C order arrives at CBOE microseconds too late, the 300 shares at $100.02 might be gone, and you might be forced to pay $100.05. This technological arms race forces SOR designers to be incredibly sophisticated, often adding artificial delays (measured in microseconds) to the orders sent to nearby exchanges so that all child orders arrive at their varying destinations at the exact same moment-a strategy known as "latency leveling."

In summary, an aggressive market order is not a simple handshake. It is a synchronized raid on fragmented pools of liquidity, battling against the geometry of the order book and the physics of light.

6.2 Scenario: The Passive Limit Order

In the previous scenario, we acted as an aggressive trader-a "taker"-willing to pay the spread to guarantee immediate execution. But what if we want to save that cost? Instead of crossing the spread to buy at the ask price, we decide to join the bid. We become a "maker" of liquidity.

This brings us to the life of a passive limit order. It is a game of patience, queue position, and a specific risk known as adverse selection.

Joining the Queue: Price-Time Priority

Imagine you want to buy shares of a company, "TechCorp." The current market is quoted as $50.00 bid and $50.05 ask. You refuse to pay the $50.05 premium. Instead, you enter a Limit Order to Buy 100 shares at $50.00.

When you click "Buy," your order travels to the exchange. The matching engine looks at the book. Since your price ($50.00) is lower than the best available selling price ($50.05), no trade occurs instantly. Instead, the engine parks your order on the bid side of the ledger.

Crucially, you are likely not the only person willing to buy at $50.00. Let us assume there are already 5,000 shares resting at that price before you arrived. In most modern equity markets, the rule is **Price-Time Priority**:

- **Price:** The best price gets filled first (highest bid, lowest offer).
- **Time:** If prices are equal, the order that arrived first gets filled first.

Your order is placed in a virtual bucket behind those 5,000 shares. You are at the back of the line. For your order to fill, sellers must cross the spread and sell at least 5,100 shares at $50.00. The first 5,000 shares sold will go to the traders ahead of you; only the subsequent shares will fill your order.

The Risk of Non-Execution

There is a distinct possibility that the market moves away from you. Suppose the news regarding TechCorp turns positive. Buyers become aggressive. They consume all the shares available at $50.05, then $50.06. The new market price shifts up to $50.10 bid / $50.15 ask.

Your order is still sitting at $50.00. You are now "behind the market." The price has run away, and you missed the trade because you insisted on saving the nickel spread. This is the opportunity cost of passive trading: the risk that while you wait for a better price, the market realizes the asset is worth more and leaves you behind.

Adverse Selection: The "Toxic" Fill

The darker risk of passive trading is the opposite scenario: you get filled, but you wish you hadn't.

Imagine your order is still sitting at the back of the queue at $50.00. Suddenly, a large institutional investor receives bad news about TechCorp. They need to sell, and they need to sell *now*. They send a massive market sell order that sweeps through the book.

They sell to the first 5,000 shares ahead of you. They sell to you. They sell to the 10,000 shares resting behind you at $49.95.

Your screen flashes "EXECUTED." You bought your shares at $50.00, exactly as you requested. However, one millisecond later, the best bid on the market drops to $49.90. You have immediately lost money.

This phenomenon is called **Adverse Selection**. In market microstructure theory, it is often summarized by a cynical rule of thumb: *If you post a limit order and everyone rushes to trade with you, you are probably on the wrong side of the trade.*

When you trade passively, you do not control *when* the trade happens; the aggressor does. If the aggressor is an informed trader (someone who knows the price is about to crash), your passive order acts as a "sitting duck." You capture the spread only when the market is quiet or mean-reverting; when the market trends hard, you are often run over.

6.3 Scenario: The Closing Auction Imbalance

If you observe a volume chart for any major stock index or widely held company, you will notice a distinct pattern. The day often begins with a burst of activity at the open, settles into a rhythmic lull during the lunch hours, and then accelerates as the afternoon wears on. But the most dramatic feature is almost always the very last second of the trading day. At exactly 4:00:00 PM ET, a massive vertical bar appears on the volume chart, representing millions of shares changing hands in a single instant.

This is the **Closing Print**. It is not a glitch, nor is it a coincidence. It is the result of the **Closing Auction**, a specialized mechanism distinct from the continuous trading we discussed earlier. While the continuous market prioritizes speed and matches orders immediately as they arrive, the auction prioritizes volume. It is designed to resolve the chaotic accumulation of end-of-day supply and demand into a single, fair benchmark price.

Why Stop Continuous Trading?

To understand the auction, we must first understand the problem it solves. Mutual funds, index funds, and ETFs manage trillions of dollars of assets. Many of these funds are mandated to track the daily performance of an index (like the S&P 500). To do this accurately, they need to buy or sell shares at exactly the closing price of the day.

If these funds tried to trade during continuous trading at 3:59 PM, their massive orders would wipe out the order book, causing prices to swing wildly. A fund buying 500,000 shares might pay $100.00 for the first share and $105.00 for the last, creating massive slippage.

The exchange solves this by effectively pressing "pause" on the continuous matching logic for specific types of orders. Instead of matching immediately, the exchange collects these orders in a bucket. This period is often called the accumulation phase.

Accumulating Interest

During the accumulation phase, traders submit special orders:

- **Market-On-Close (MOC):** "Buy shares at whatever the closing price turns out to be." These traders do not care about the price; they care about guaranteed execution at the benchmark.

- **Limit-On-Close (LOC):** "Buy shares at the closing price, but only if that price is $100 or lower."

As 4:00 PM approaches, the matching engine looks at this pile of buy and sell interest. It does not match them one by one. Instead, it performs a mathematical calculation to solve for X: What single price will allow the maximum number of shares to trade?

Solving for the Clearing Price

This calculation is an exercise in finding equilibrium. The engine constructs a theoretical supply curve and a demand curve based on all the orders in the bucket.

- **The Buyer's Perspective:** At a low price, demand is high because everyone wants a bargain. As the potential clearing price moves up, limit buy orders drop out, and demand decreases.

- **The Seller's Perspective:** At a low price, supply is low because few want to sell. As the price moves up, more limit sellers are willing to participate, and supply increases.

The engine overlays these two curves. The point where they intersect, or come closest to intersecting, is the price where supply meets demand most efficiently. This is known as the **Clearing Price**.

At this specific price, the exchange can pair the maximum possible number of buy shares with sell shares.

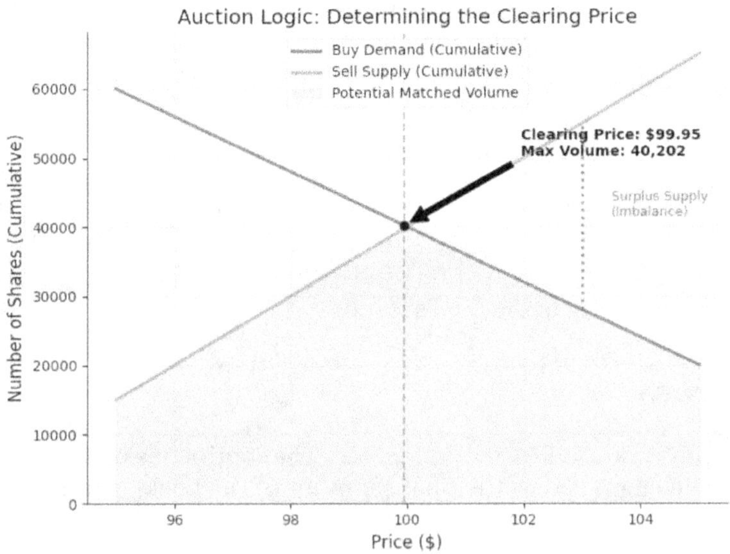

As illustrated in the chart, the matching engine seeks the peak of the "Matched Volume" area.

- If the price is set too low (left side of the chart), there is huge demand but very little supply. Only the small amount of supply can be traded.
- If the price is set too high (right side of the chart), there is huge supply but no buyers. Only the small amount of demand can be traded.
- At the intersection, the overlap is maximized.

The Imbalance and the Freeze

Rarely do the buy and sell sides balance perfectly. Even at the optimal price, there might be 500,000 shares to buy and only 450,000 shares to sell. This difference is the **Imbalance**.

In the minutes leading up to the close (typically from 3:50 PM to 4:00 PM), the exchange broadcasts this imbalance information to the public data feeds. They effectively announce: *"We have a purchase surplus of 50,000 shares at the current anticipated price. Does anyone want to sell?"*

This is a call to high-frequency traders and institutional desks to step in. If a trader sees a "Buy Imbalance," they know there is excess demand. They might send a "Sell On Close" order to fill that gap, capturing the liquidity and helping to stabilize the price. This interaction between the published imbalance and the traders reacting to it is what causes the flurry of activity in the final seconds.

The Cross

At precisely 4:00:00 PM, the gate closes. The continuous market shuts down. The engine takes the final snapshot of the book, confirms the clearing price, and executes the cross.

In a singular microsecond event, millions of shares are matched. The 500,000 buy orders and the 450,000 sell orders (plus the 50,000 late-arriving sellers who responded to the imbalance) all trade instantly at the single Clearing Price.

This single event prints to the tape as one aggregate trade record, causing the massive volume spike seen on daily charts. For the participants, it is the ultimate moment of liquidity: huge positions are entered or exited without the price moving against them during the trade, because everyone transacted at the mathematically optimal equilibrium point.

6.4 Measuring Quality and Avoiding Pitfalls

After dissecting how orders sweep through routers, sit in queues, or converge in auctions, we arrive at the most practical question for any investor: "Did I get a good trade?"

In the physical world, quality is easy to spot. If you buy an apple, you can check if it is bruised. In financial markets, execution quality is more abstract. You hit "Buy," and seconds later, you own the shares. But between that click and the confirmation, money can be saved or lost in fractions of a penny. Understanding how to measure this performance separates sophisticated traders from those who simply hope for the best.

Price Improvement and the Effective Spread

The most common benchmark for a trade is the National Best Bid and Offer (NBBO). As we discussed earlier, this represents the absolute best price currently displayed on public exchanges.

If stock XYZ is offered at $100.05, and you submit a market order to buy, you expect to pay $100.05. However, you might look at your trade confirmation and see a price of $100.045 or even $100.04. This implies you bought the stock for less than the seller was publicly asking.

This phenomenon is called **Price Improvement**. It occurs because not all liquidity is displayed on the public "lit" markets. Your broker's Smart Order Router (SOR) may have sent your order to a wholesaler or a dark pool that was willing to beat the public exchange price to take the other side of your trade. While saving a penny per share sounds trivial on a small order, these savings compound significantly over a lifetime of investing.

To measure this scientifically, finance professionals use a metric called the **Effective Spread**.

Imagine the market is $100.00 bid and $100.10 offer. The midpoint of that market is $100.05.

- If you buy at the offer ($100.10), you have paid 5 cents more than the midpoint.
- If you receive price improvement and buy at $100.08, you only paid 3 cents more than the midpoint.

Your effective spread is narrower in the second scenario. By comparing the price you actually paid against the midpoint of the market at the exact moment your order arrived, you can strip away market noise and see strictly how much the "friction" of trading cost you.

The Myth of the Rigged Market

While getting a better price is a pleasant surprise, failing to get a fill at all is a source of immense frustration. This often leads to one of the most pervasive myths in trading: "The market is rigged against the little guy."

Consider this common scenario: You place a Limit Order to buy 1,000 shares at $50.00. The market dips. You watch the ticker tape (the stream of executed trades) and see several trades happen at exactly $50.00. Then, the price rallies to $50.50. Your order sits unfilled.

It is natural to feel cheated. You saw trades happen at your price, so why didn't you participate? Before assuming conspiracy, we must look at the mechanical realities of the matching engine we explored earlier.

The Queue and the Bus Stop

The first reason for a missed fill is simply **Queue Priority**. As discussed in the section on passive orders, limit orders are processed First-In-First-Out (FIFO). Those trades you saw executing at $50.00 likely belonged to traders who joined the queue minutes or hours before you. They were at the front of the line; you were at the back. The sellers ran out of stock before the matching engine reached your position in the queue.

The Odd-Lot Problem

The second reason is regulatory. In the United States, the "protected" quotes that establish the NBBO are generally based on "round lots"-typically 100 shares.

If a high-frequency trader or a retail investor sells 13 shares at $50.00, that trade will print to the tape. You will see "$50.00" flash on your screen. However, your order for 1,000 shares cannot be satisfied by 13 shares, and depending on the specific order instructions and exchange rules, your broker might not have matched you against that tiny fragment of liquidity. Seeing a price on a screen does not guarantee there was enough volume at that price to fill your order.

The Speed of Light

Finally, we must account for **Latency**. The market data feed on a standard retail trading platform is incredibly fast, but it is not instantaneous. By the time the pixels on your monitor light up to show a trade at $50.00, that event has already happened in the past.

In a fast-moving market, an algorithm might cancel its sell order at $50.00 and re-post it at $50.01 in microseconds. Your human eyes see $50.00, and your finger clicks "Buy," but you are shooting at a ghost. The order is rejected or rests unfilled not because the game is rigged, but because the information you acted upon was stale by the time it reached the exchange.

By understanding these mechanics-price improvement, spread capture, queue priority, and latency-we move from a conspiratorial view of the markets to a structural one. The machine is not malicious; it is simply rigid, following a strict set of logic gates that process millions of requests with deterministic precision.

6.5 Rules of the Road: Integrity and Regulation

Throughout this chapter, we have journeyed through the micro-events that constitute a trade. We have seen how a Smart Order Router navigates a fragmented landscape, how a limit order waits its turn in a digital queue, and how the closing auction resolves the day's chaos into a single price. To the uninitiated, this high-speed environment can resemble the Wild West—a place where speed is the only law and the fastest gun always wins.

However, the reality is starkly different. The modern stock market is perhaps the most heavily regulated and codified ecosystem in the financial world. While the machinery operates in microseconds, the framework that governs it is rigid, explicit, and publicly available. Understanding this framework is the final key to demystifying the "black box." It ensures that while the market may be fast and sometimes ruthless, it is not random.

The Constitution of the Exchange: The Rulebook

When we think of an exchange like the NYSE or Nasdaq, we often think of them as technology companies. While true, they are legally defined as Self-Regulatory Organizations (SROs). This designation carries a heavy burden: they must police their own markets and strictly adhere to a set of rules filed with government regulators (such as the Securities and Exchange Commission in the United States).

Every behavior described in this book-from how a peg order floats, to how a tie-breaker is resolved in an auction, to the exact hierarchy of the order book-is written down in the exchange's **Rulebook**.

For a trader, the rulebook is the law of the land. If an exchange's matching engine behaves in a way that contradicts its rulebook, the exchange can be fined heavily, and the trades may be broken (cancelled). This provides a critical guarantee to market participants: **determinism**.

If you place an order, you should be able to predict exactly how the matching engine will handle it, provided you know the state of the order book. There are no "judgment calls" made by the computer. If your order was skipped, it wasn't because the machine didn't like you; it was because of a specific logic gate defined in Rule 4751 (or similar) regarding order priority or risk constraints.

The Glue of the Market: Reg NMS

In the scenario regarding aggressive execution, we discussed how a Smart Order Router (SOR) splits a large order and sends pieces to different exchanges to capture the best price. You might have wondered: *Why do they bother? Why not just buy everything at the easiest exchange, even if the price is a penny worse?*

The answer lies in a landmark piece of regulation known as **Regulation National Market System (Reg NMS)**, specifically the **Order Protection Rule**.

In simple terms, this rule states that a trade cannot occur at a price worse than the best displayed price on another exchange. If Exchange A has shares for sale at $100.00, Exchange B cannot execute a buy order at $100.01. It must either match the $100.00 price or route the order to Exchange A.

This rule acts as the "glue" that binds the fragmented liquidity pools together. It forces the scattered exchanges to behave, virtually, as a single unified market. It protects the investor: even if you send your buy order to a venue with bad prices, the system is legally obligated to prevent you from getting a bad fill if a better one is publicly available elsewhere.

Fair Access and the Level Playing Field

A common criticism of high-frequency trading and electronic markets is that the game is "rigged" against the little guy. While it is true that professional firms have advantages—faster computers, better data feeds, and teams of PhDs—the structural integrity of the market relies on the principle of **Fair Access**.

Exchanges are generally prohibited from discriminating between members. The colocation centers (where servers live) are open to anyone willing to pay the fees, and those fees must be filed publicly. The data feed that tells a high-frequency trader the price is available to any subscriber. The matching logic does not know if an order comes from a global bank or a retail brokerage; it only sees price, size, and time.

The distinction here is between *equality of outcome* and *equality of rules*. A professional runner will beat an amateur in a 100-meter dash every time, not because the track is rigged, but because they are faster. Similarly, in the market, professionals invest heavily to be faster. The regulatory framework ensures that the "track"—the matching engine and the rules of the race—is the same for everyone.

We began this book with the goal of turning the "black box" of the market into a transparent process. We have dismantled the engine to see its pistons—the matching algorithms, the order types, the auctions, and the routers.

What we find inside is not magic, nor is it a conspiracy. It is a complex system of queues and logic gates, operating at blinding speeds but constrained by rigid rules. When an order is placed, it enters a deterministic machine that processes it according to strict priority—Price, then Time. When the market closes, math takes over to maximize volume. And surrounding it all is a regulatory fence ensuring that prices are respected across venues.

For the modern investor or student of finance, the market is no longer a place of mystery. It is a mechanism. And like any mechanism, once you understand how the gears turn, you can navigate it with confidence. The noise of the ticker tape fades, replaced by the clear, rhythmic hum of the matching engine doing exactly what it was built to do.

www.ingramcontent.com/pod-product-compliance
Lightning Source LLC
LaVergne TN
LVHW022014200926
848481LV00007B/2389
* 9 7 9 8 8 9 6 6 5 2 4 5 8 *